this book belongs to:

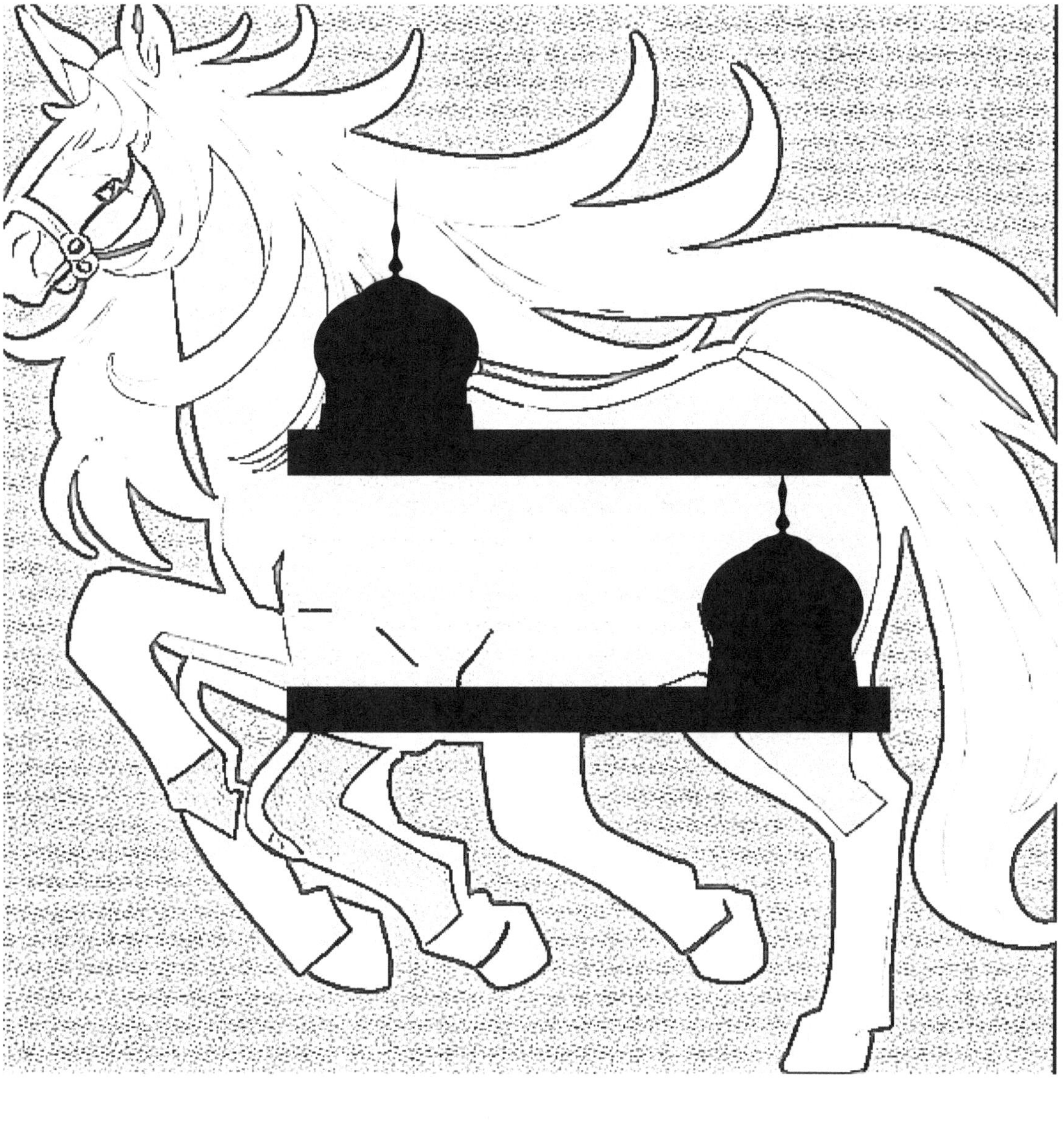

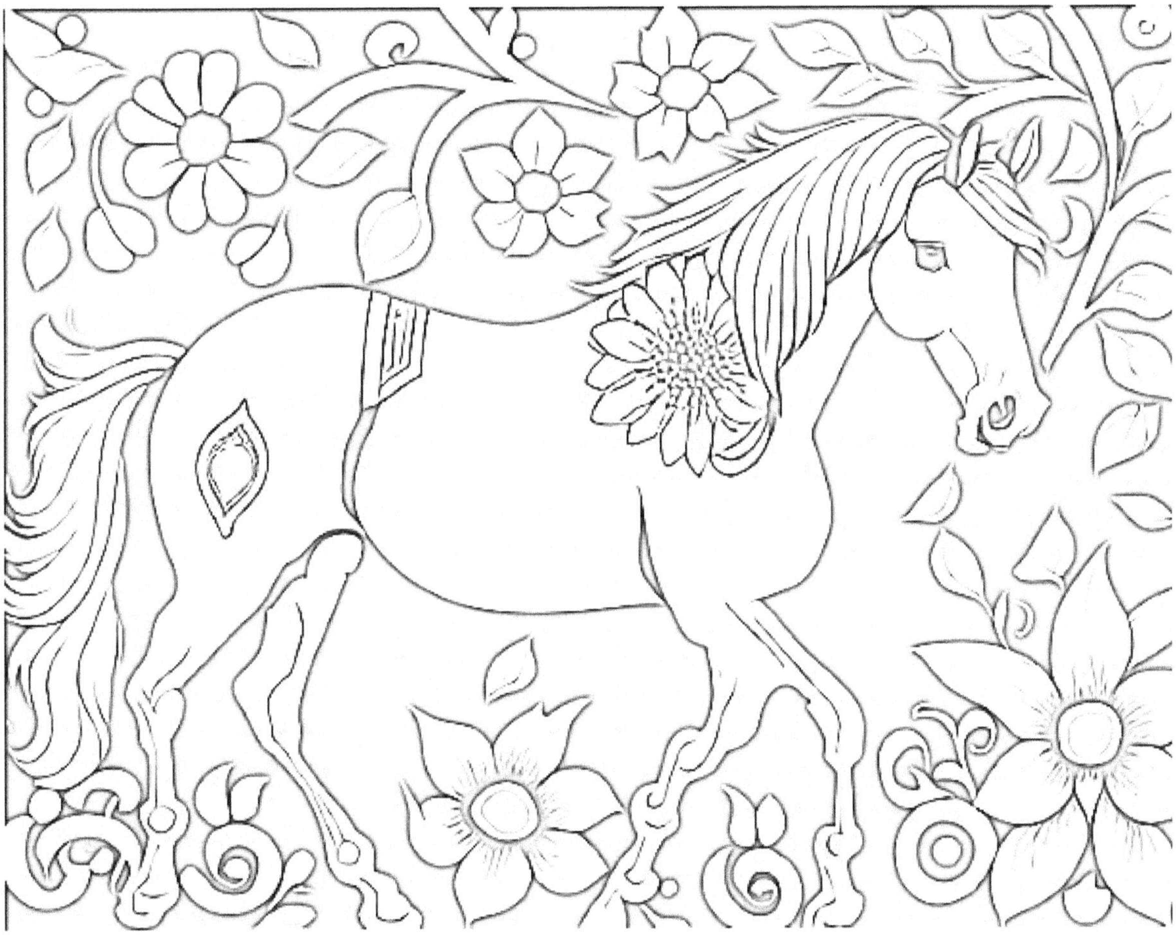

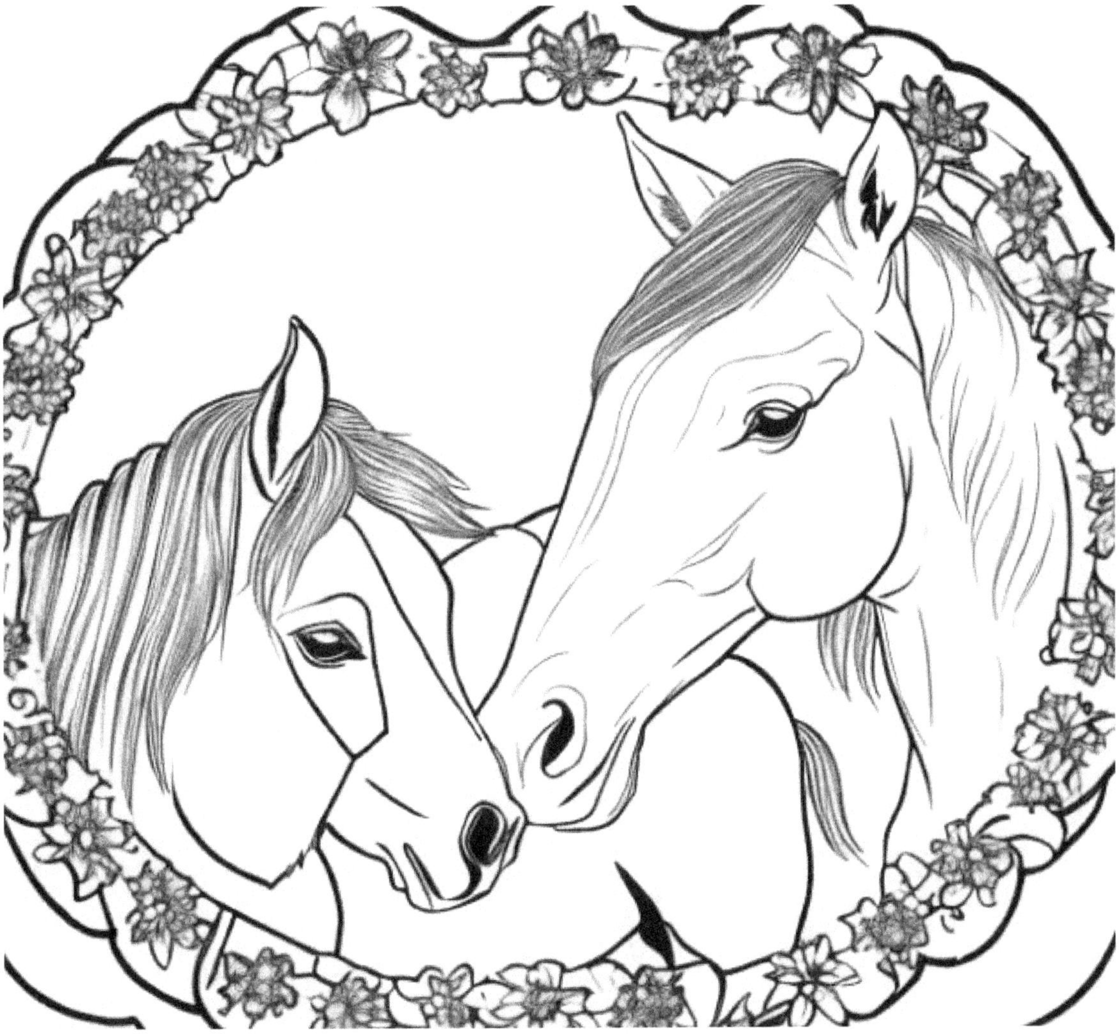

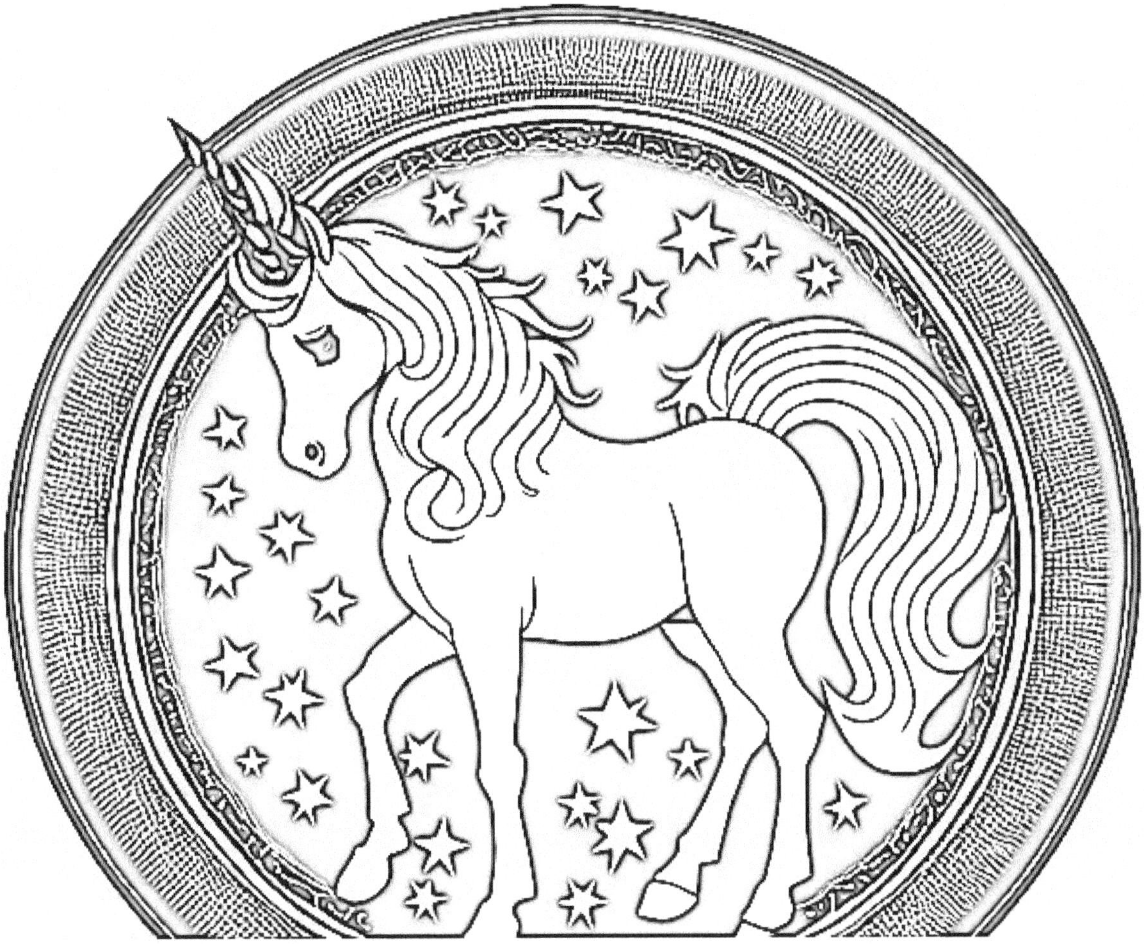

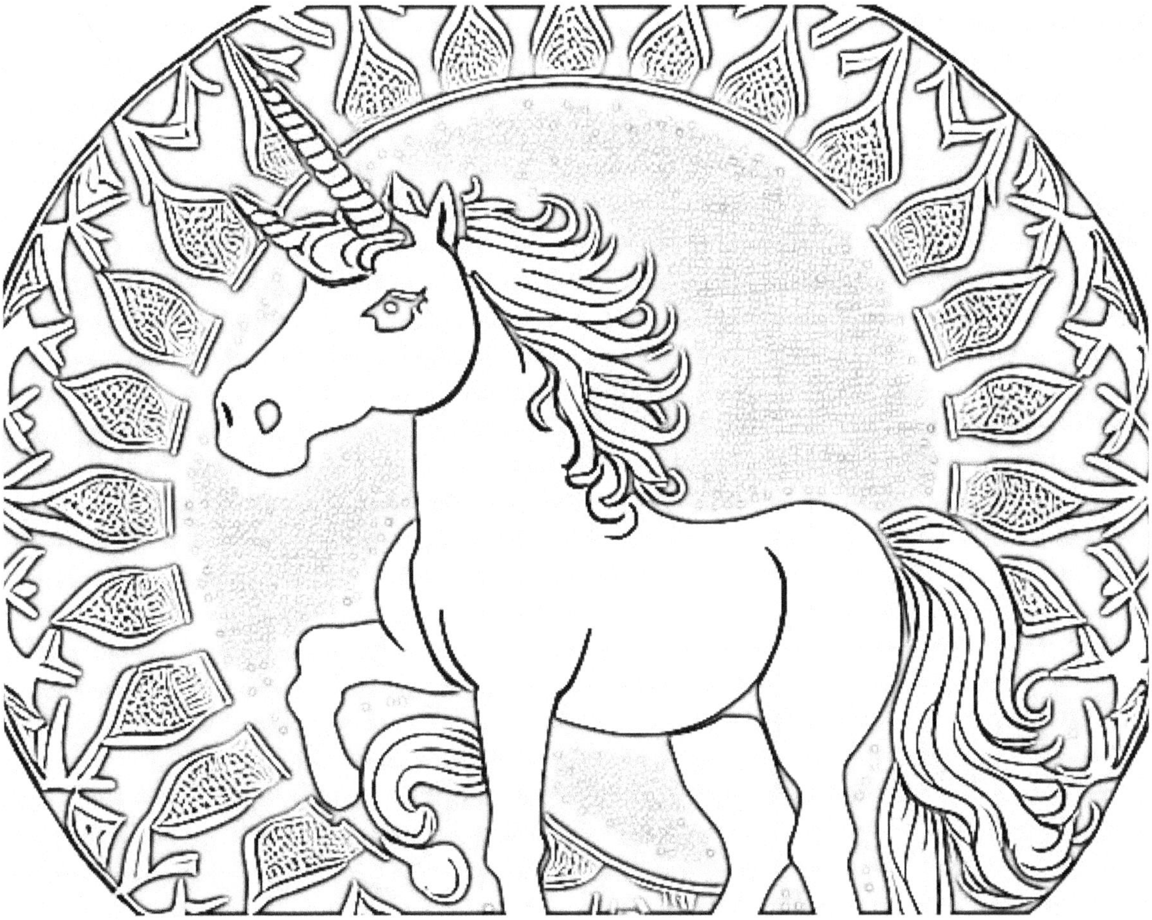

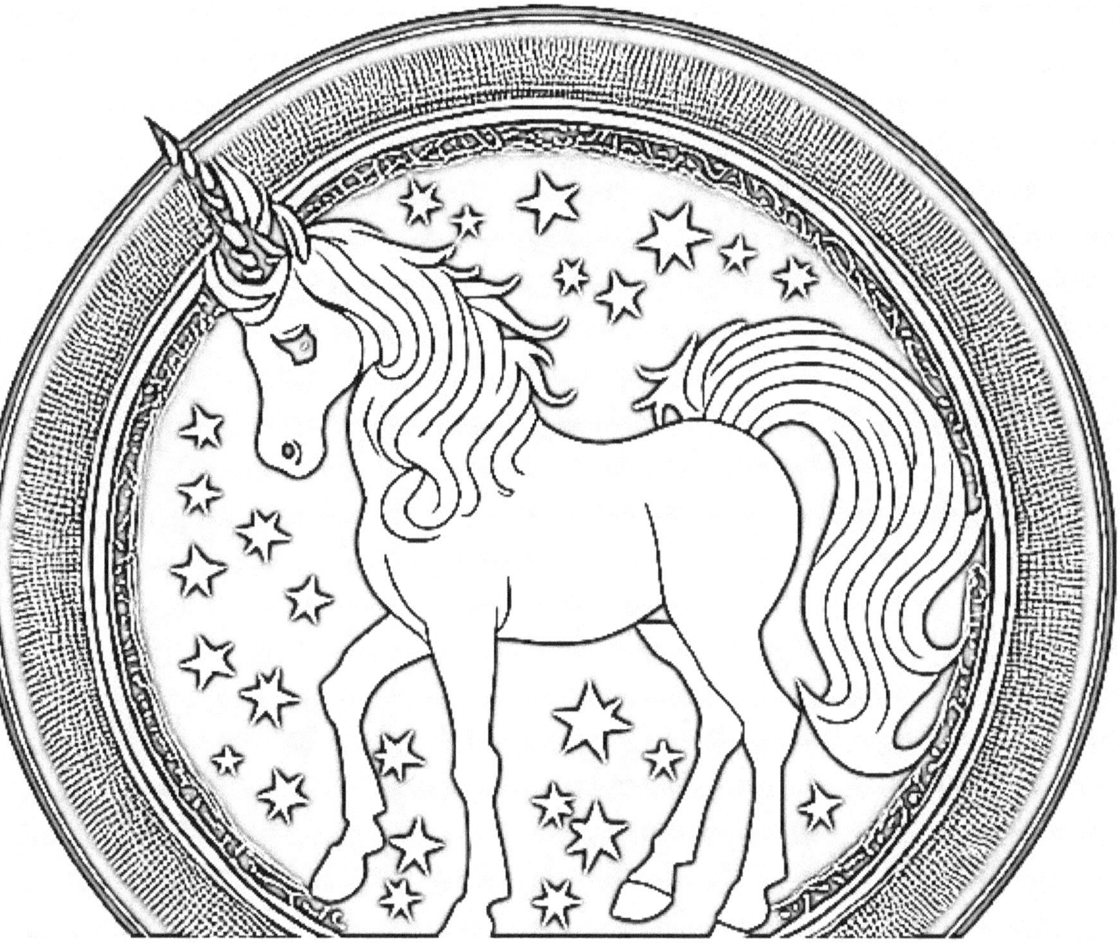

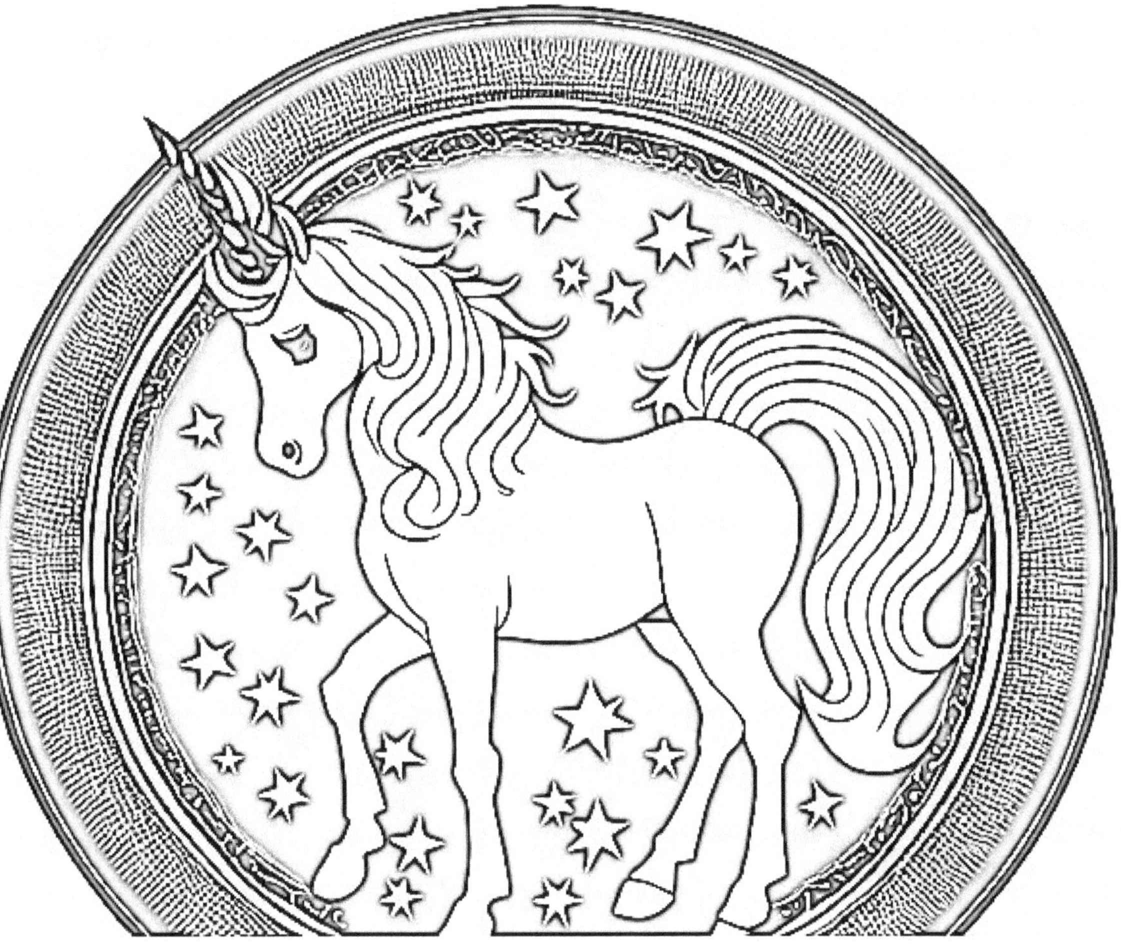

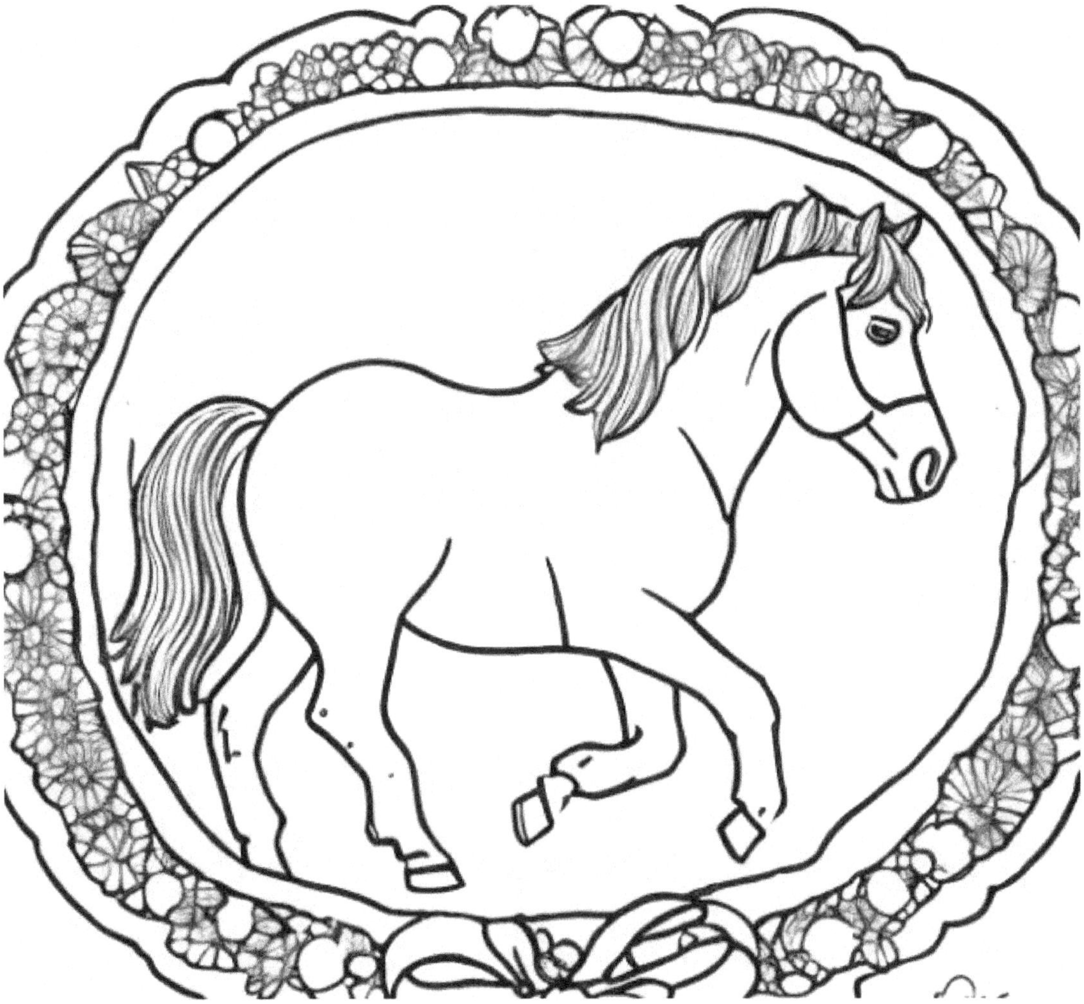

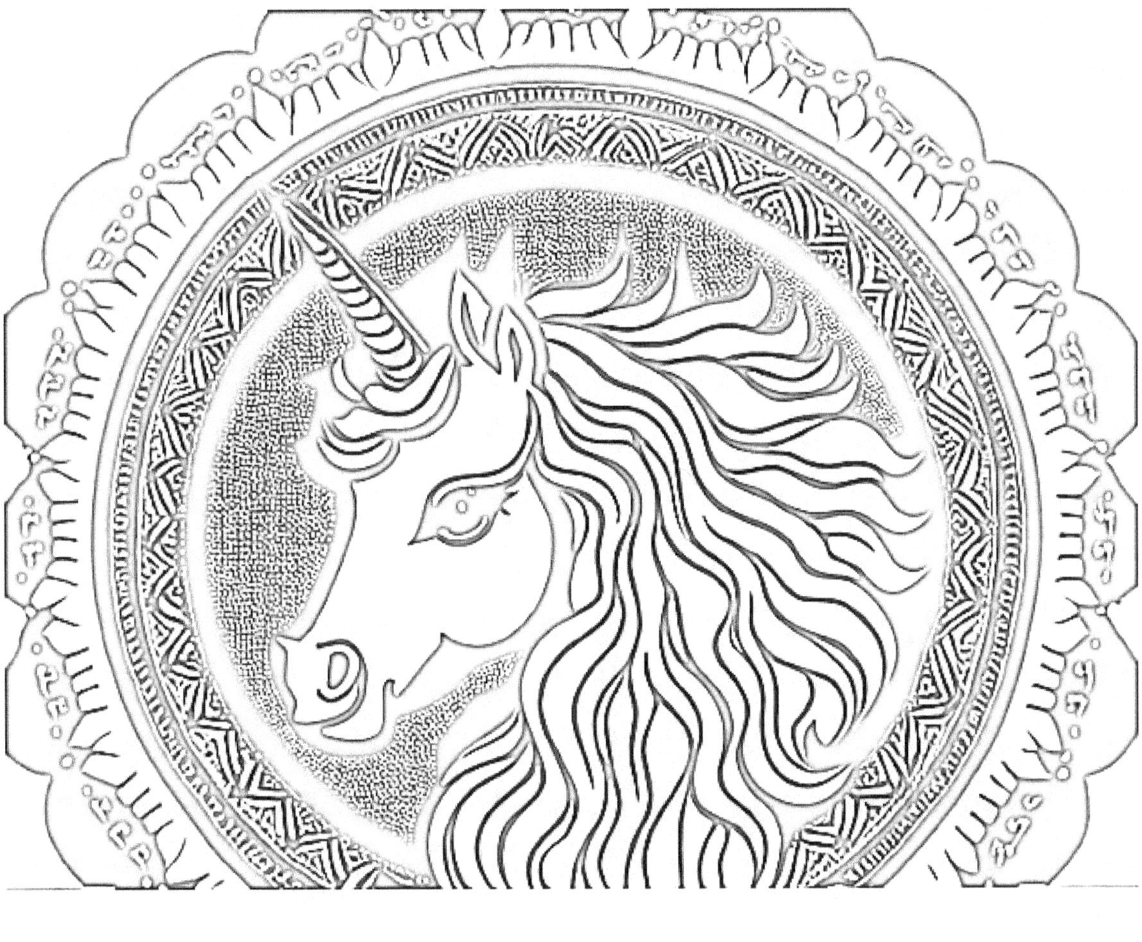

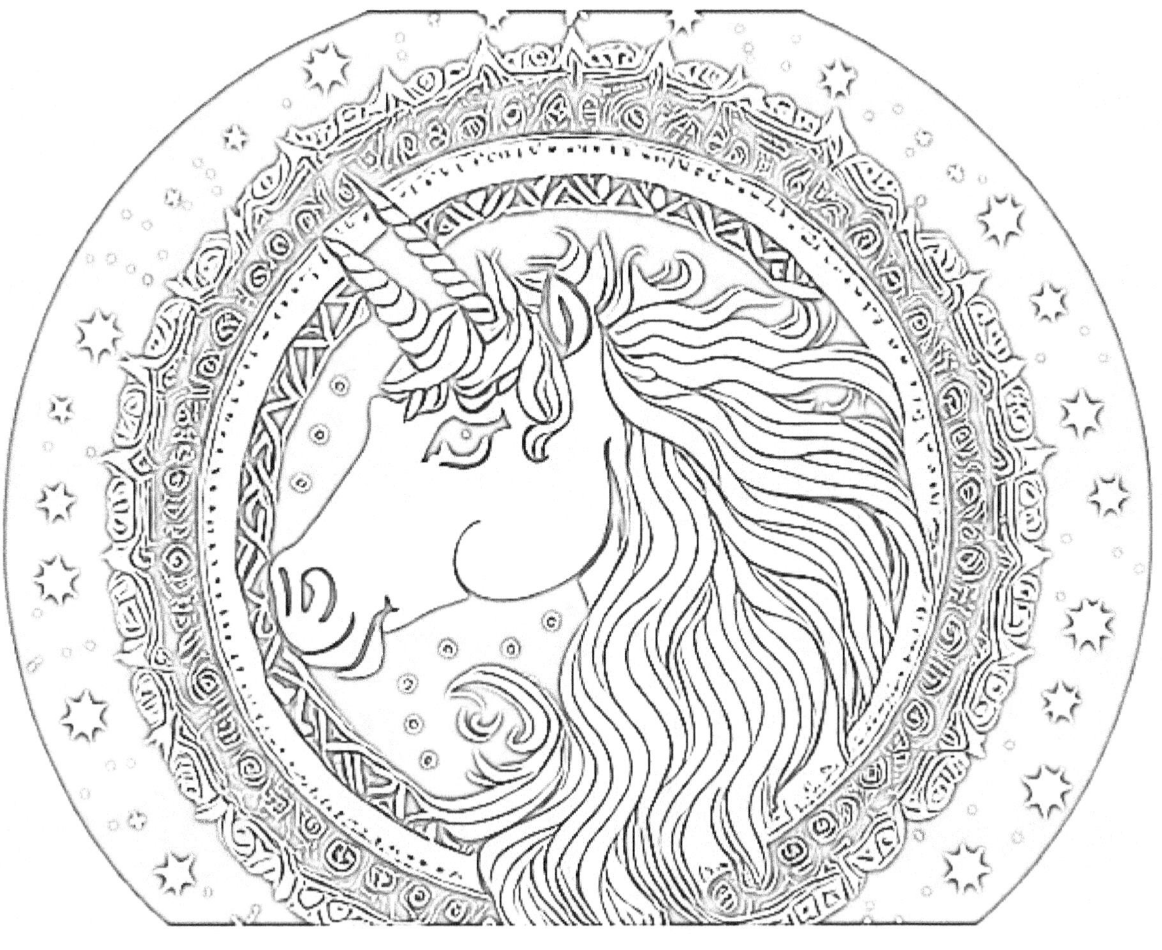

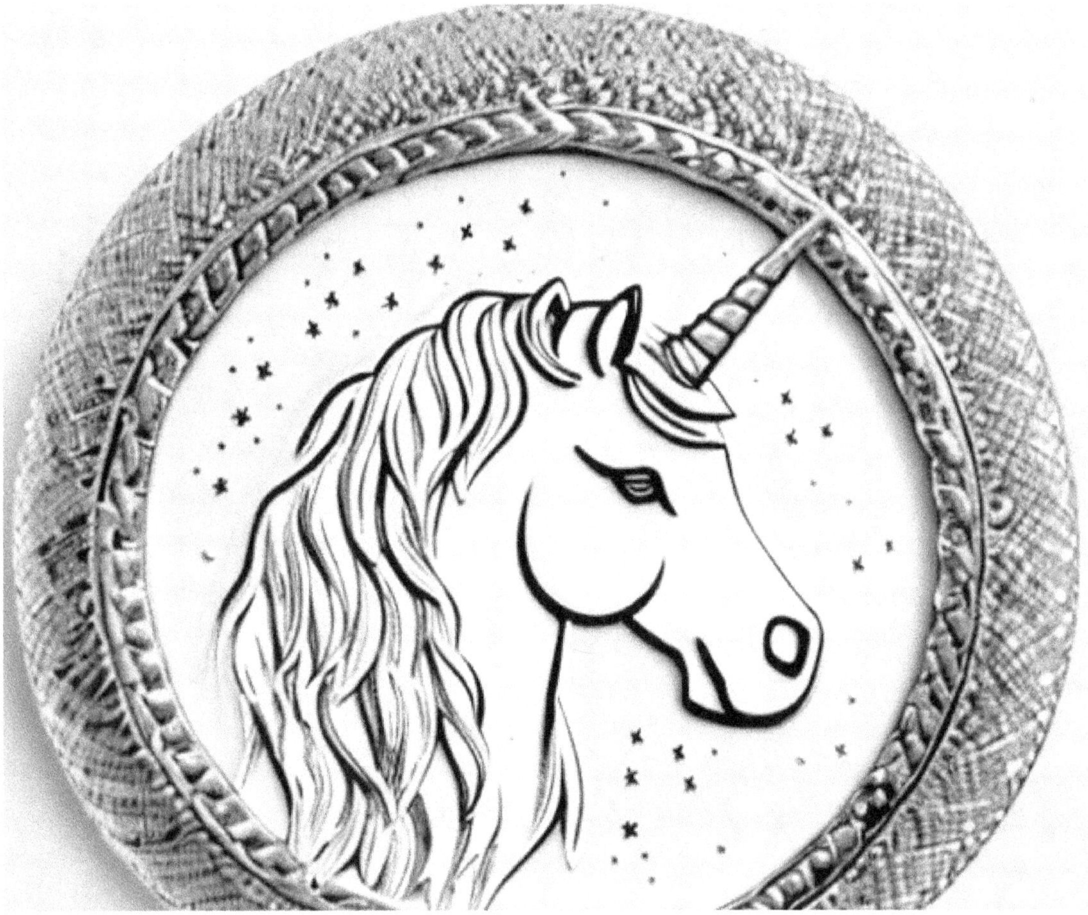

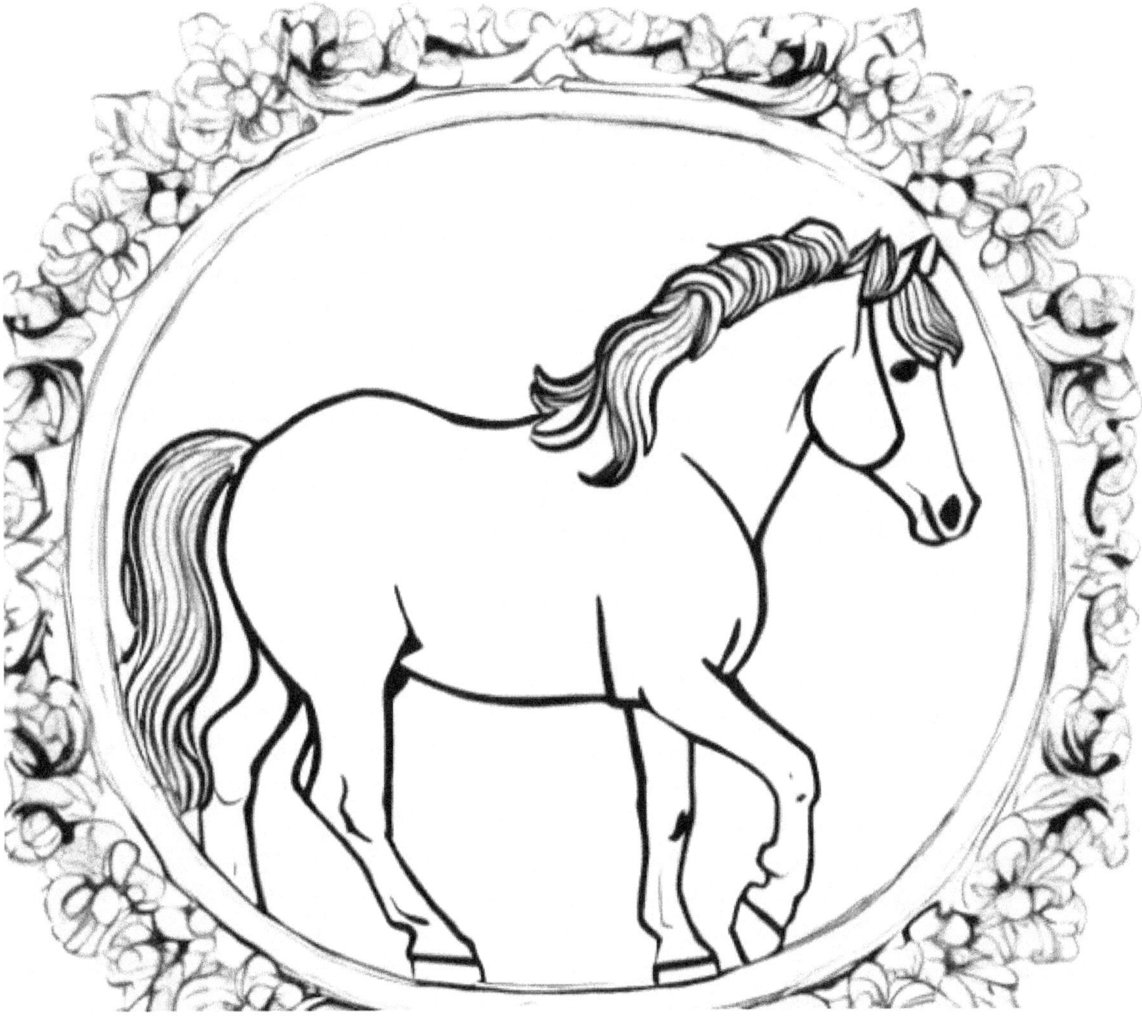

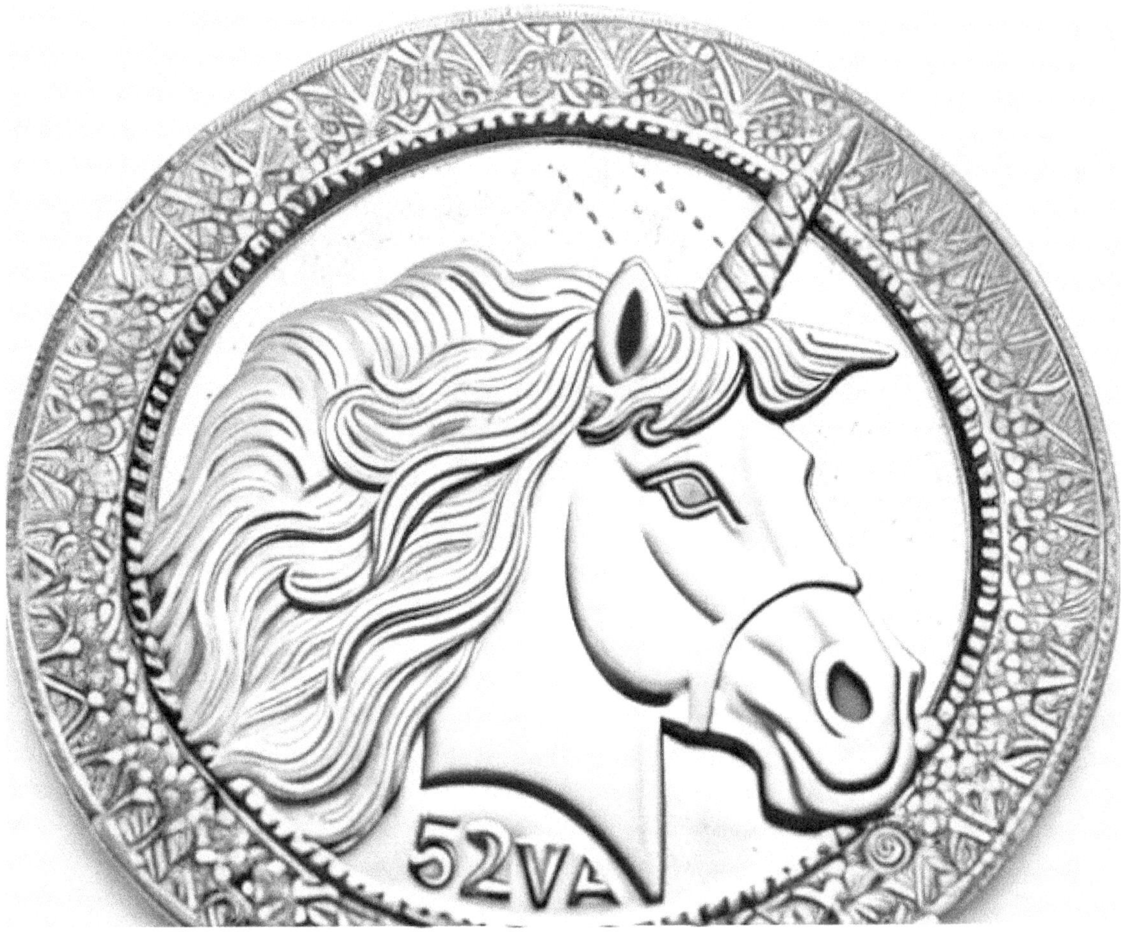
52VA

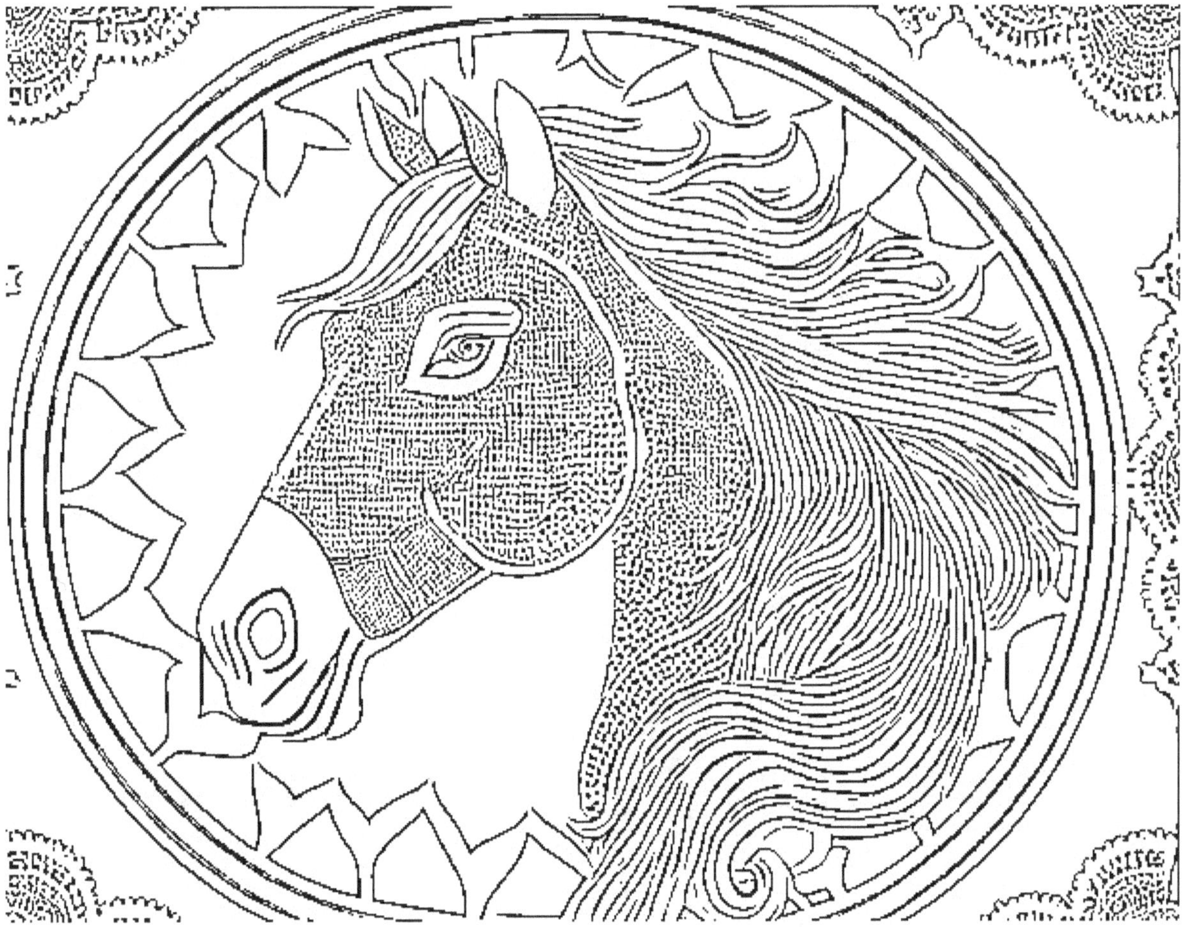

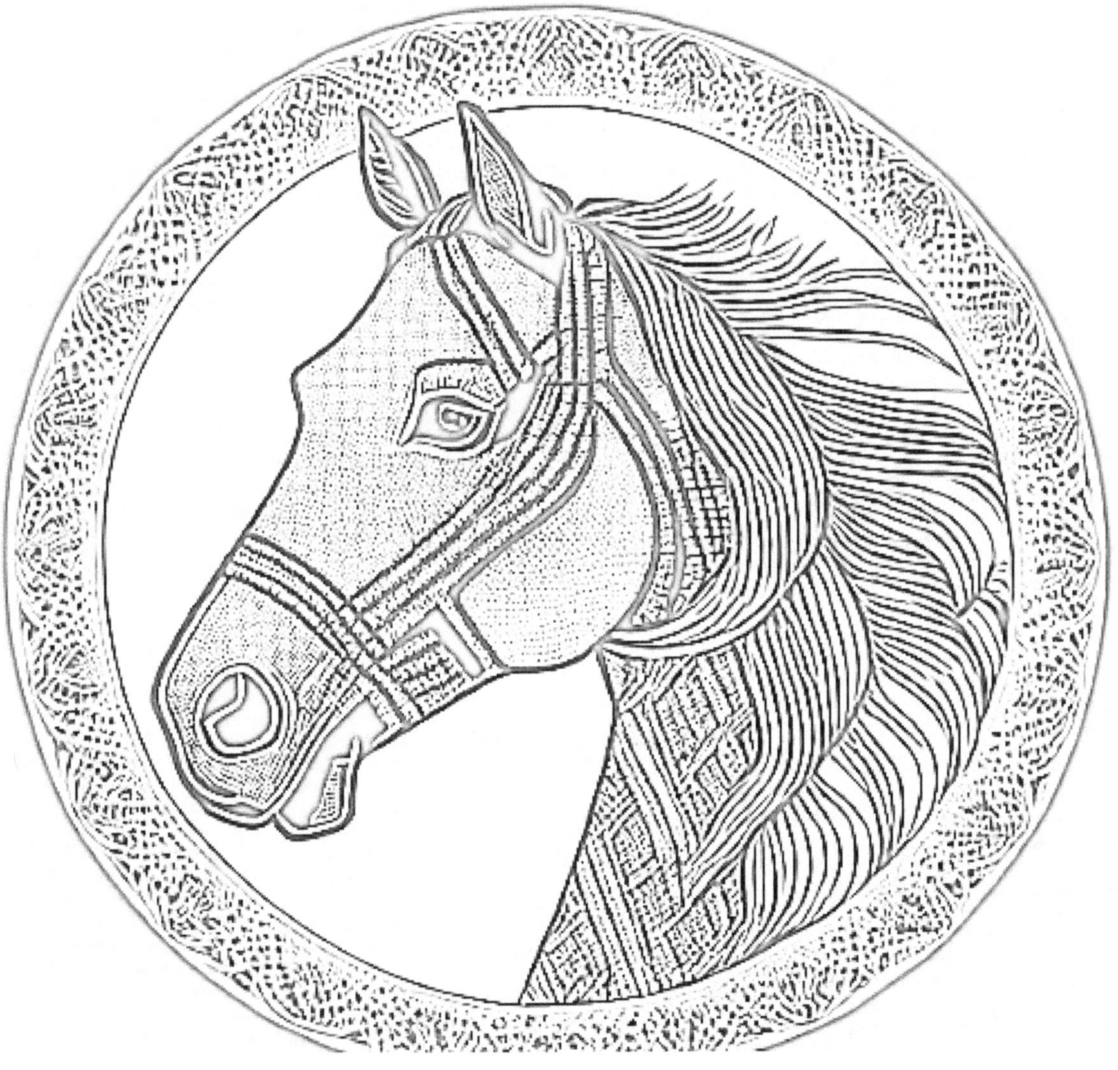

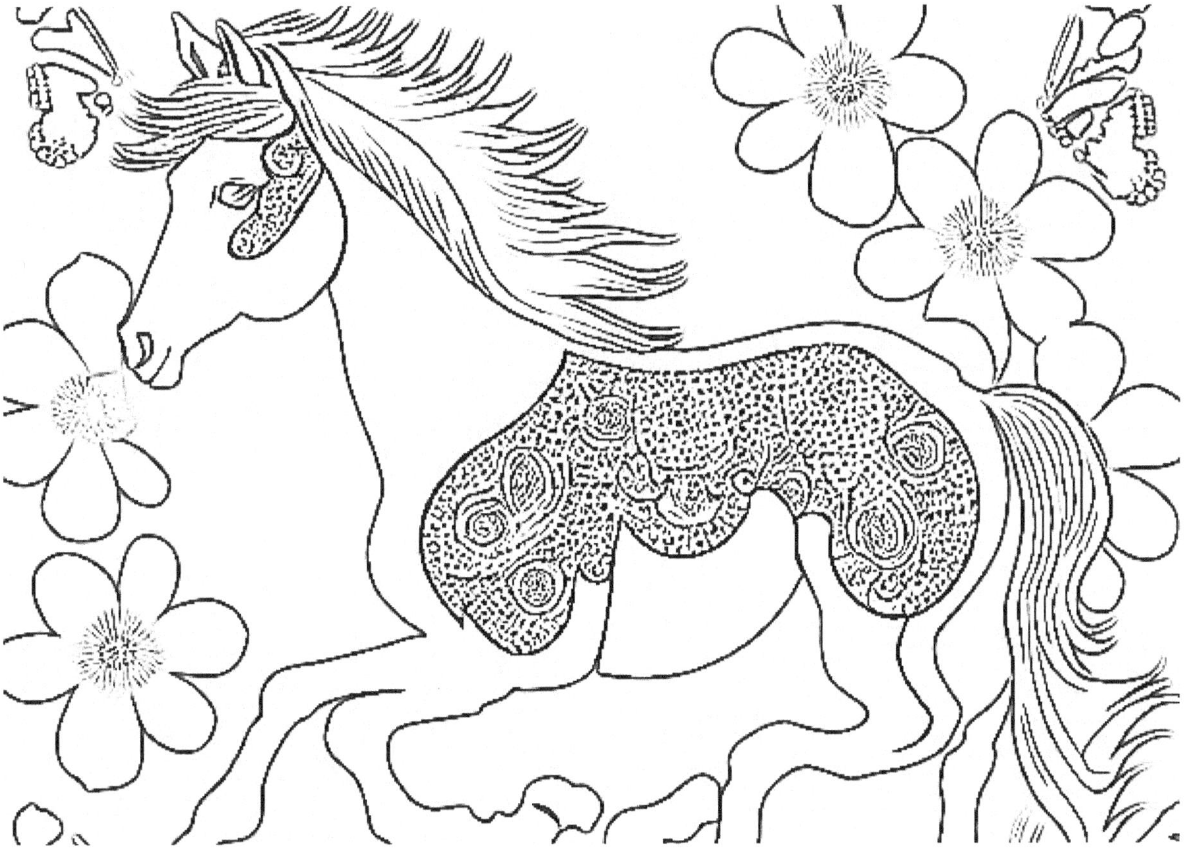

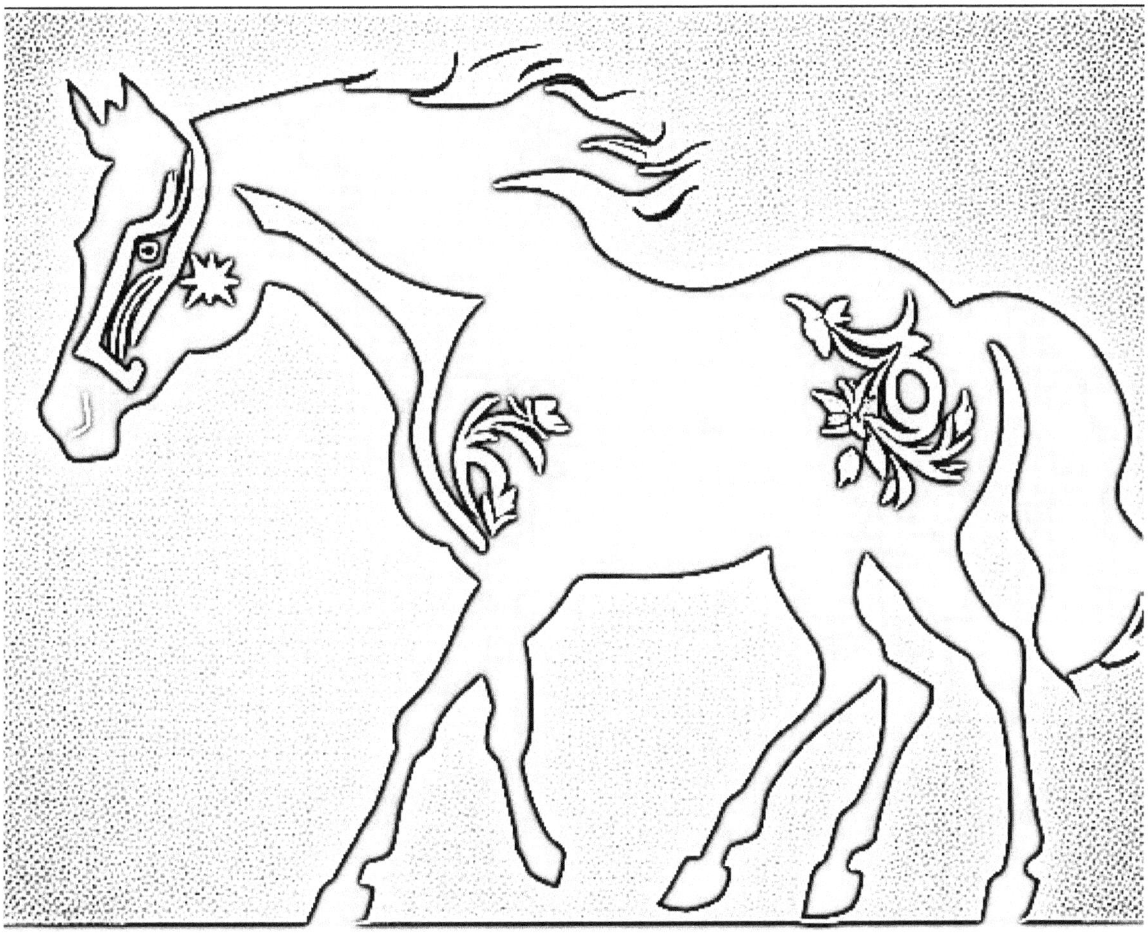

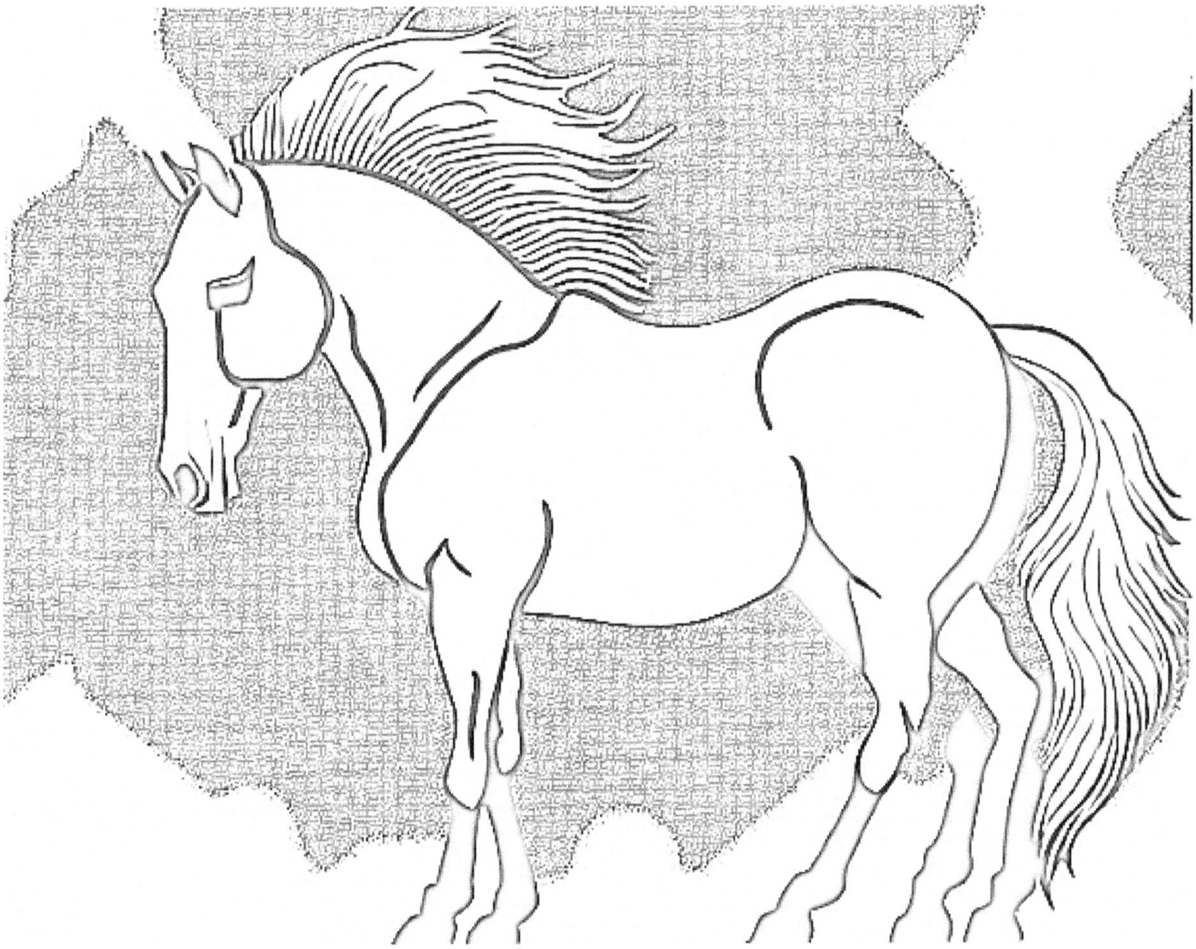

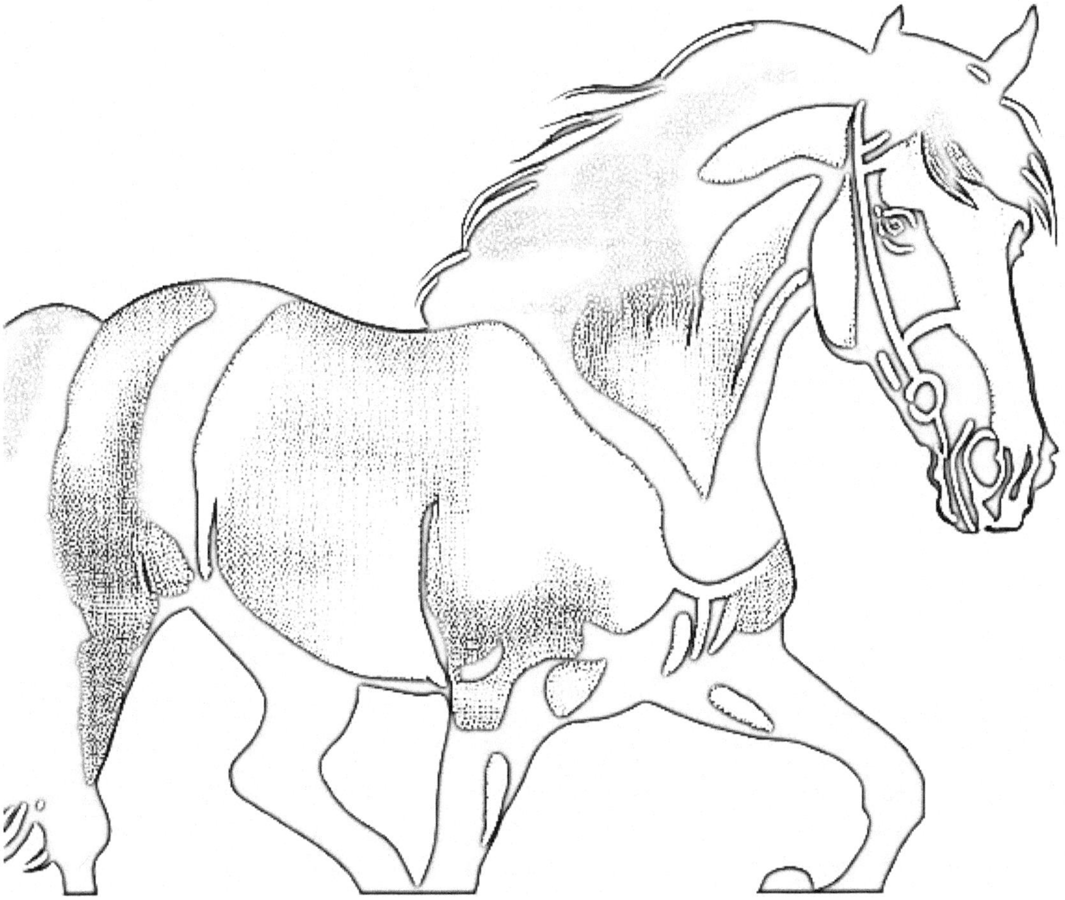

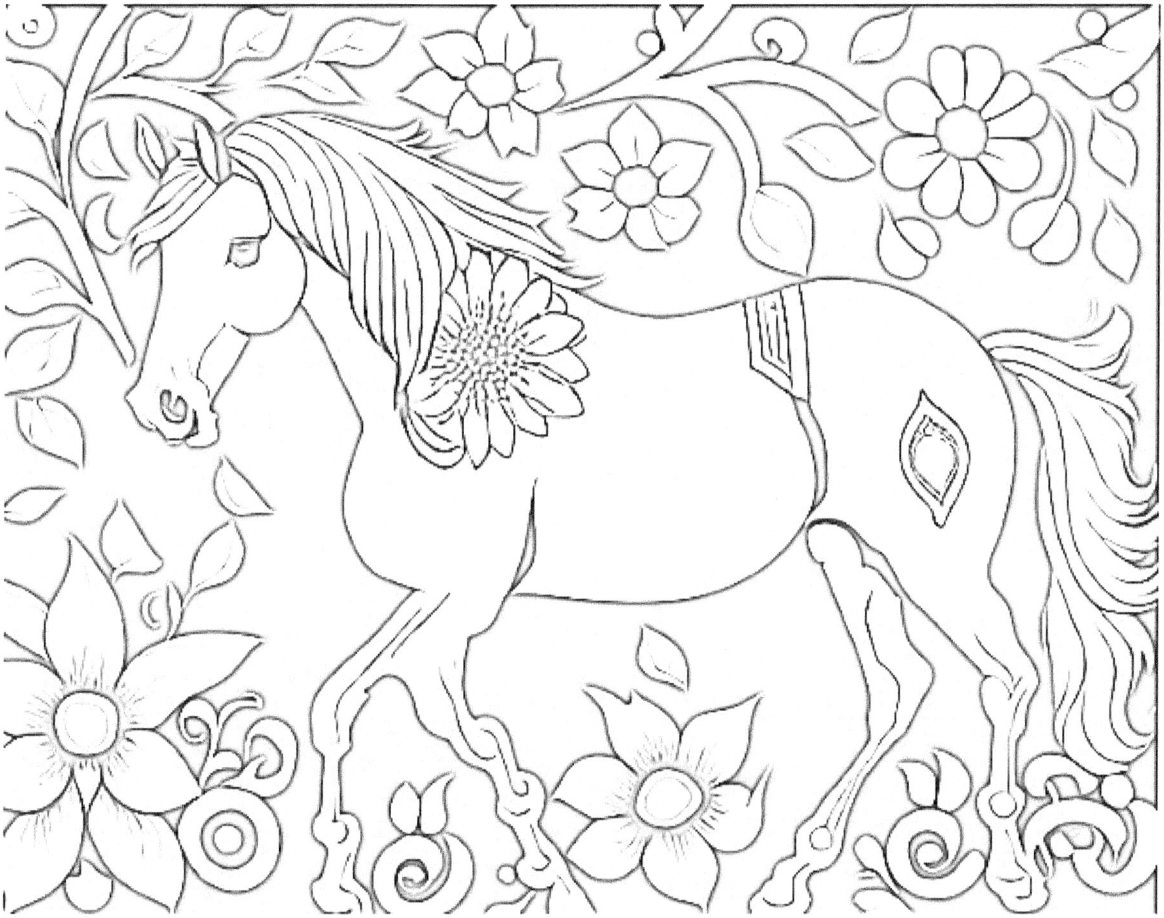

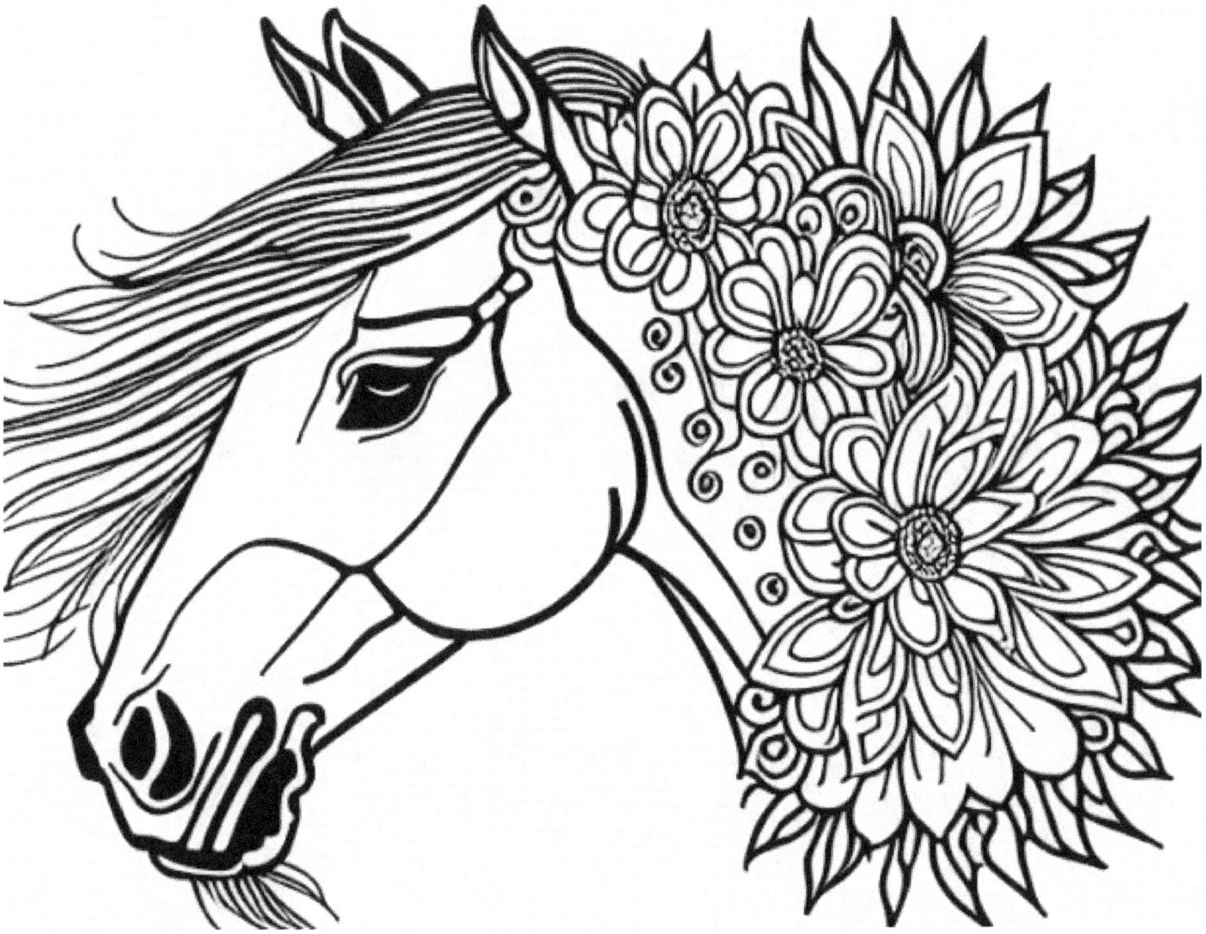

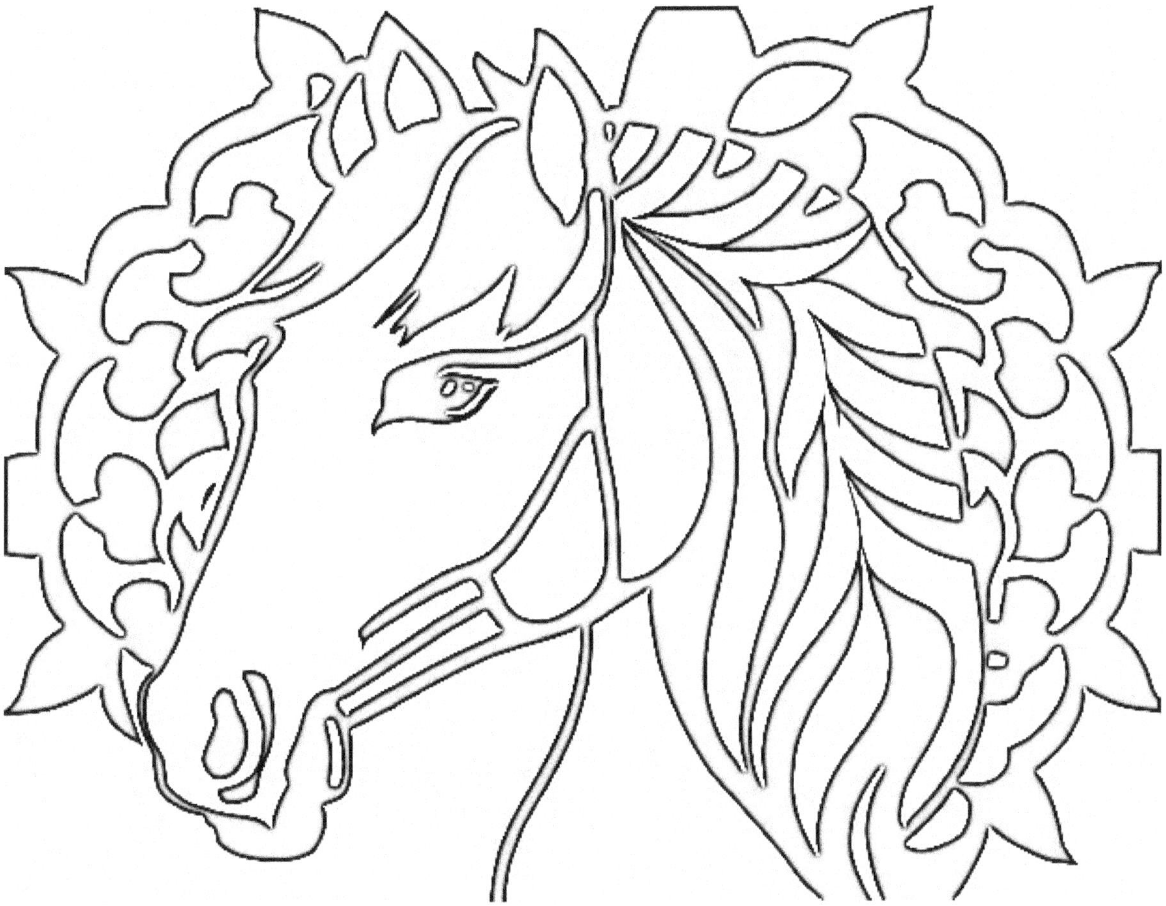

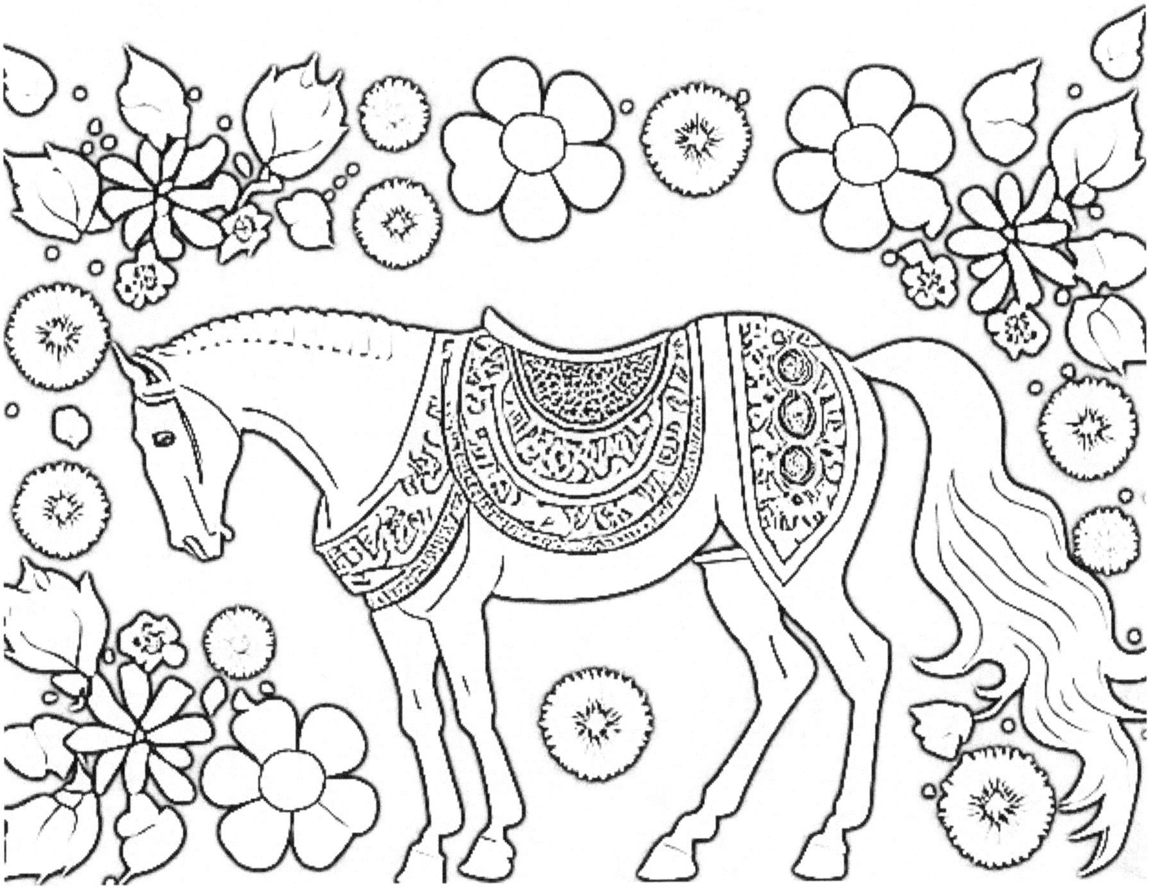

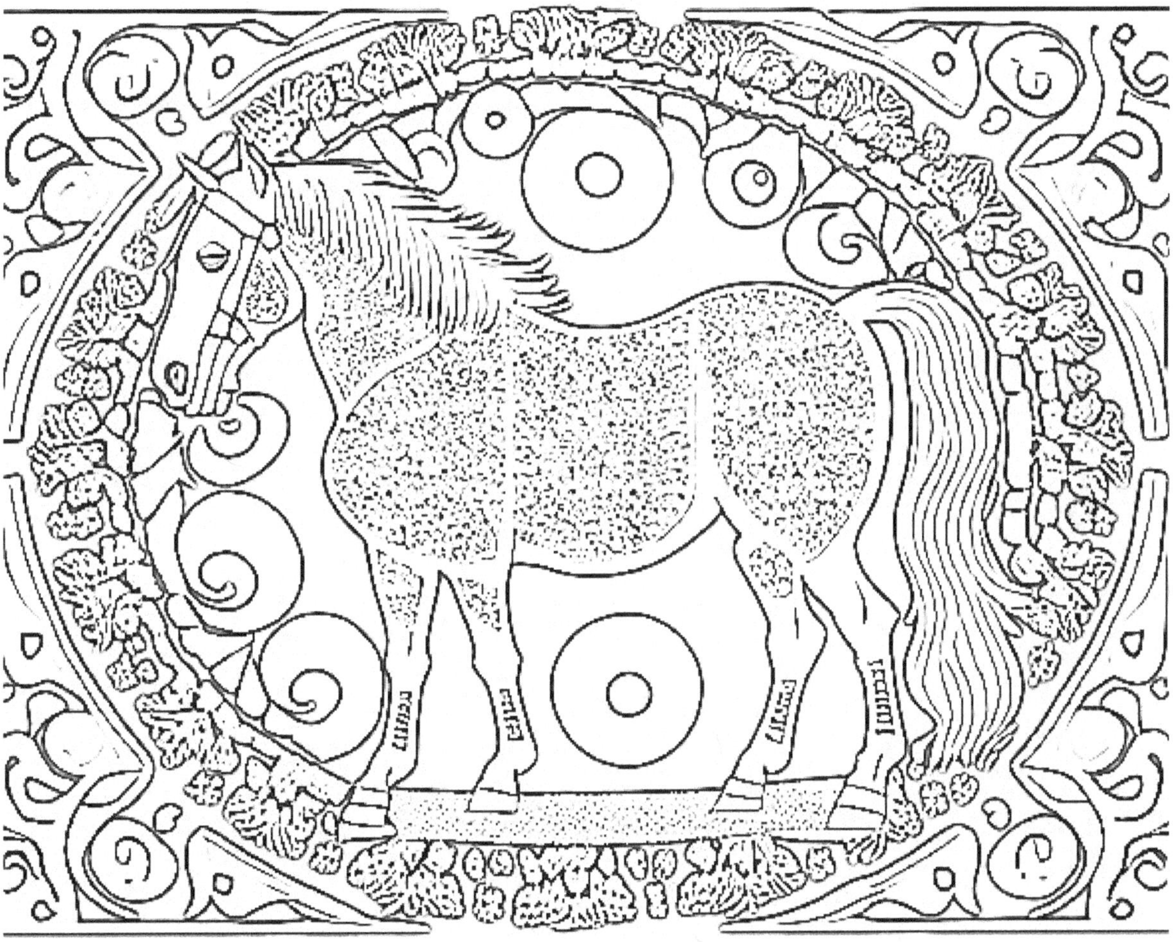

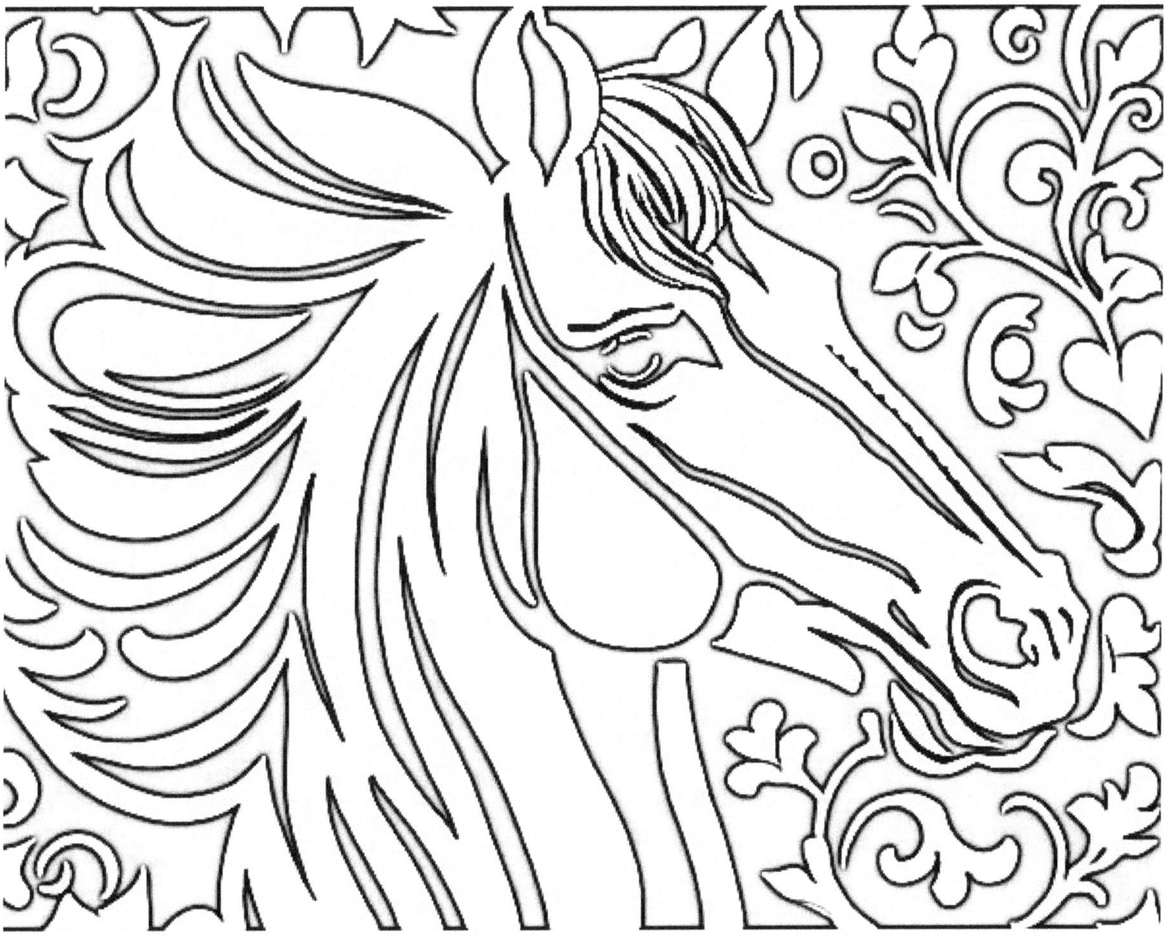

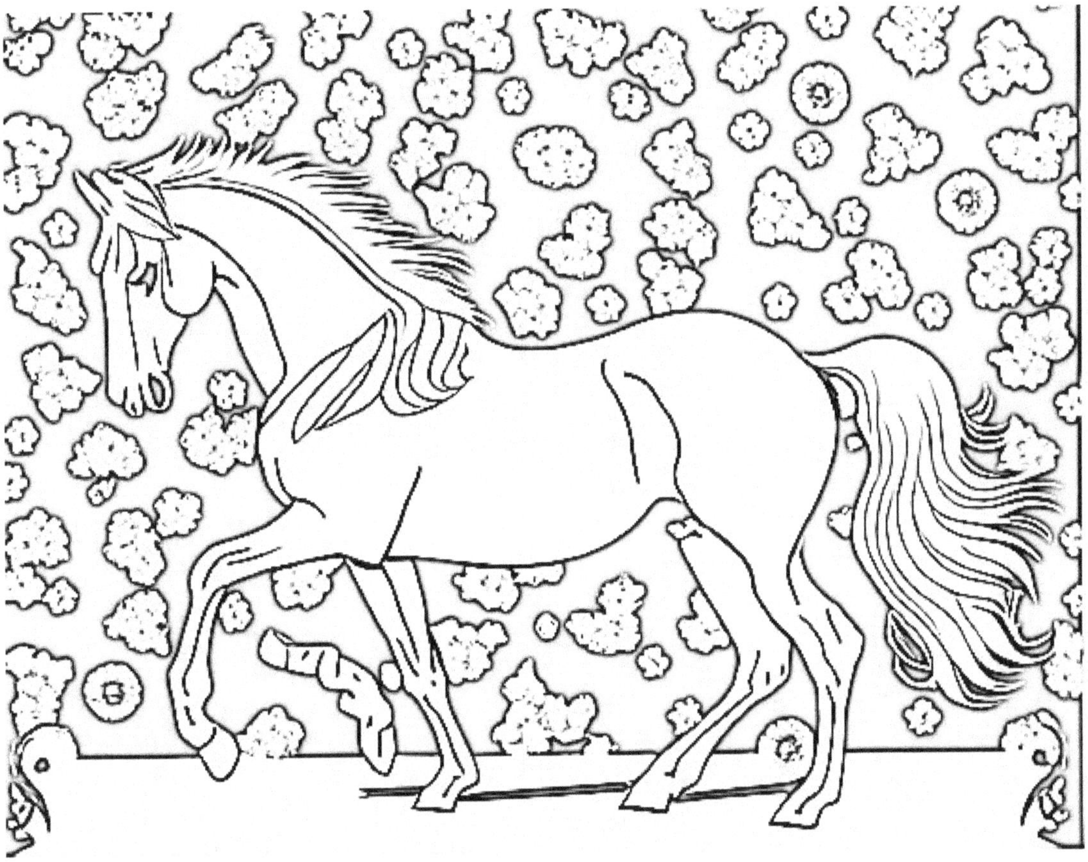

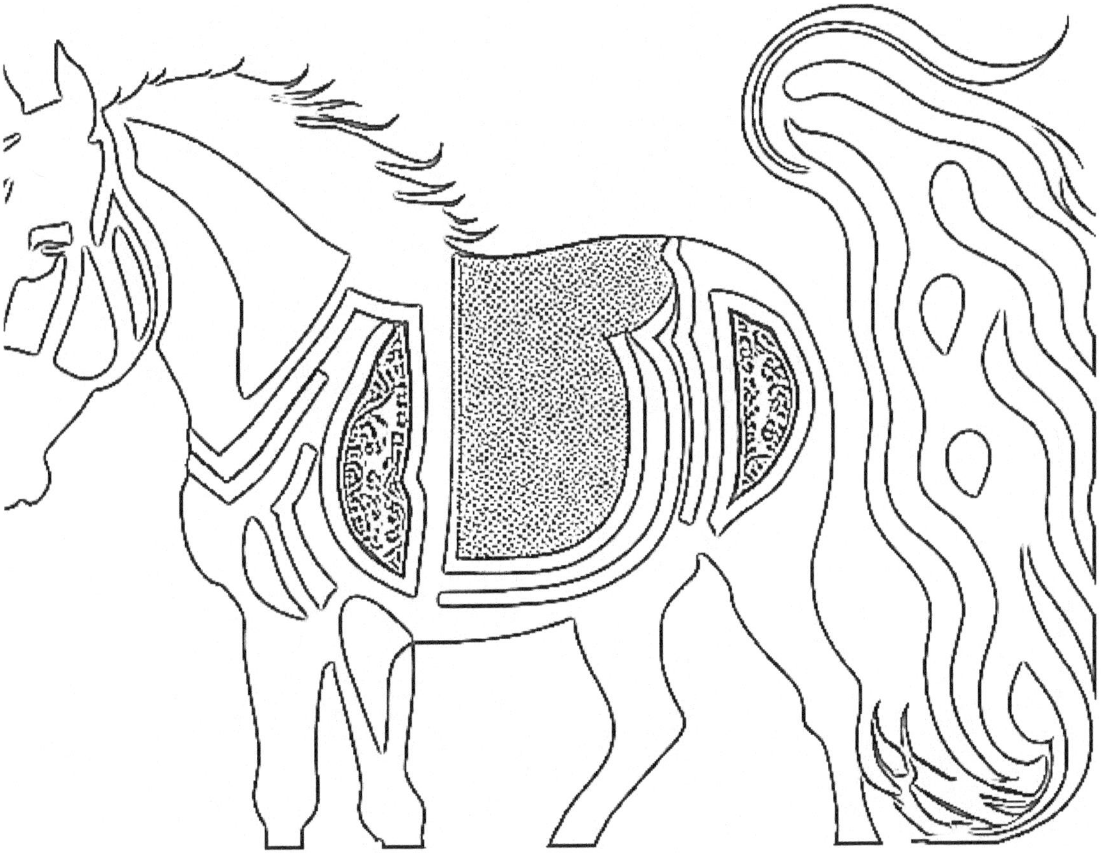

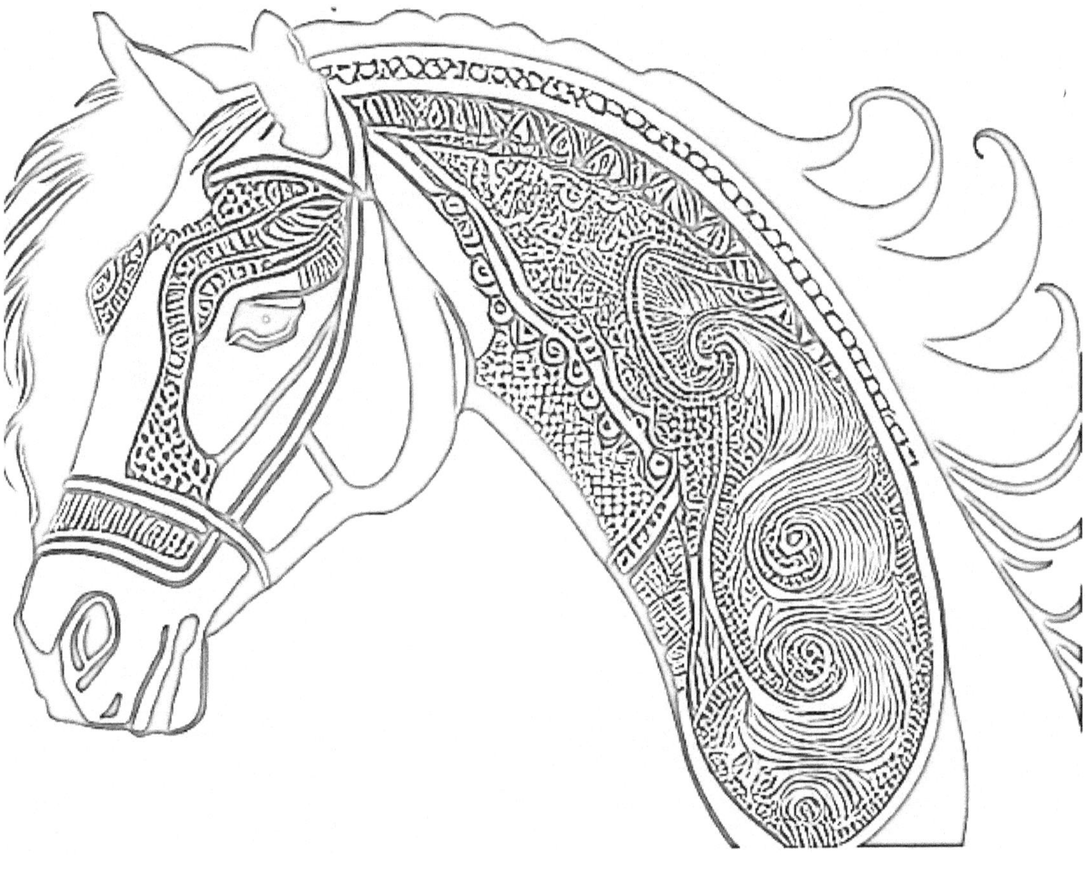

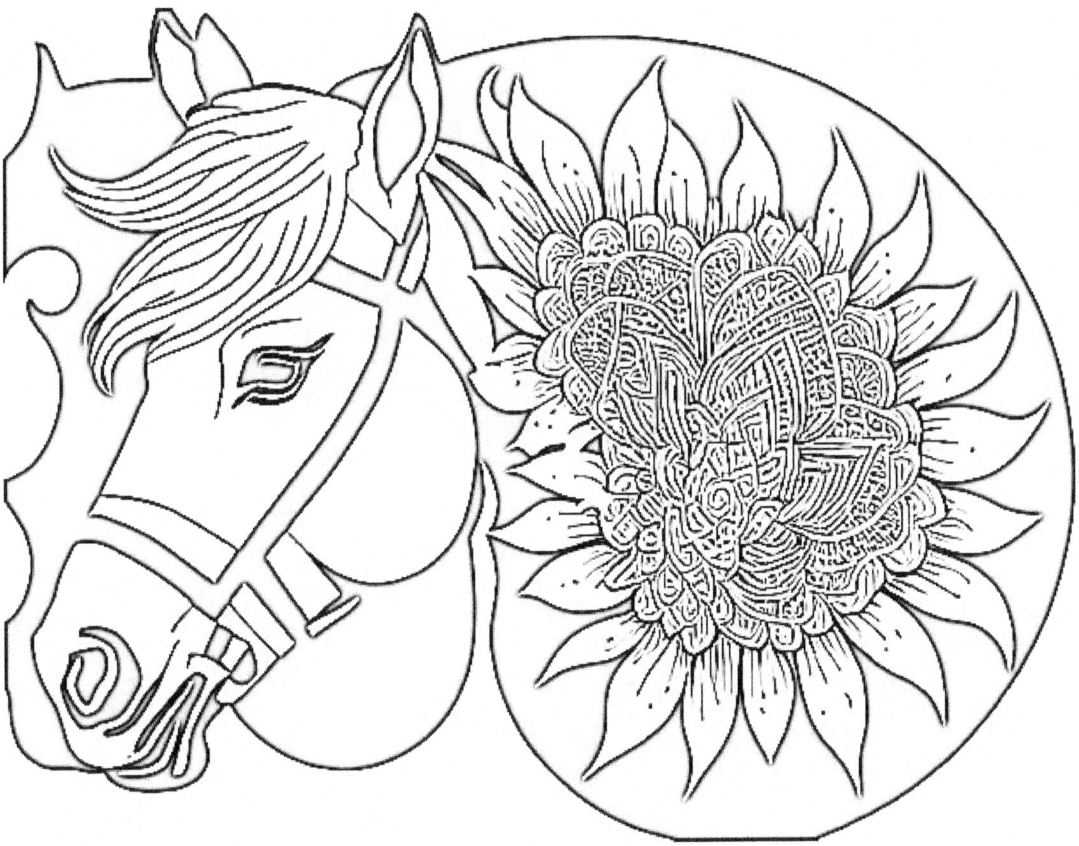

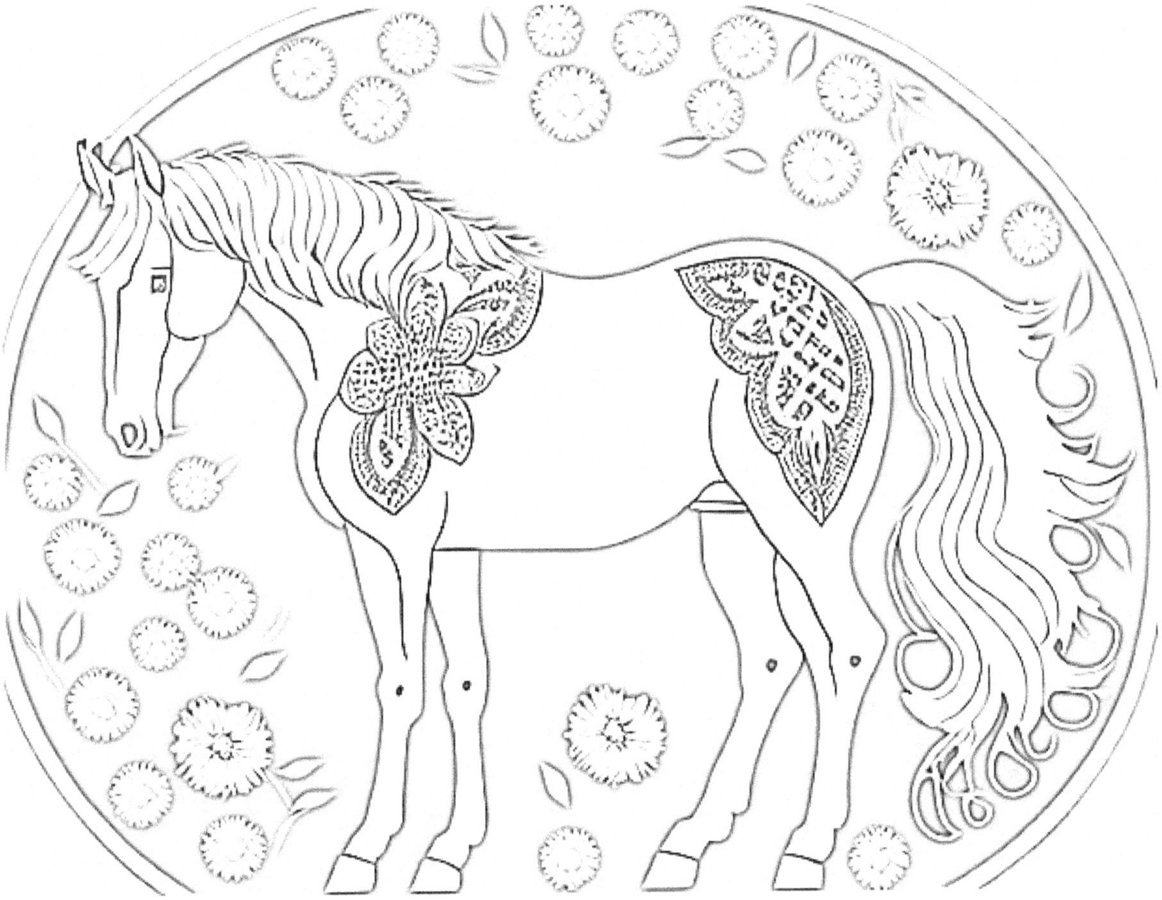

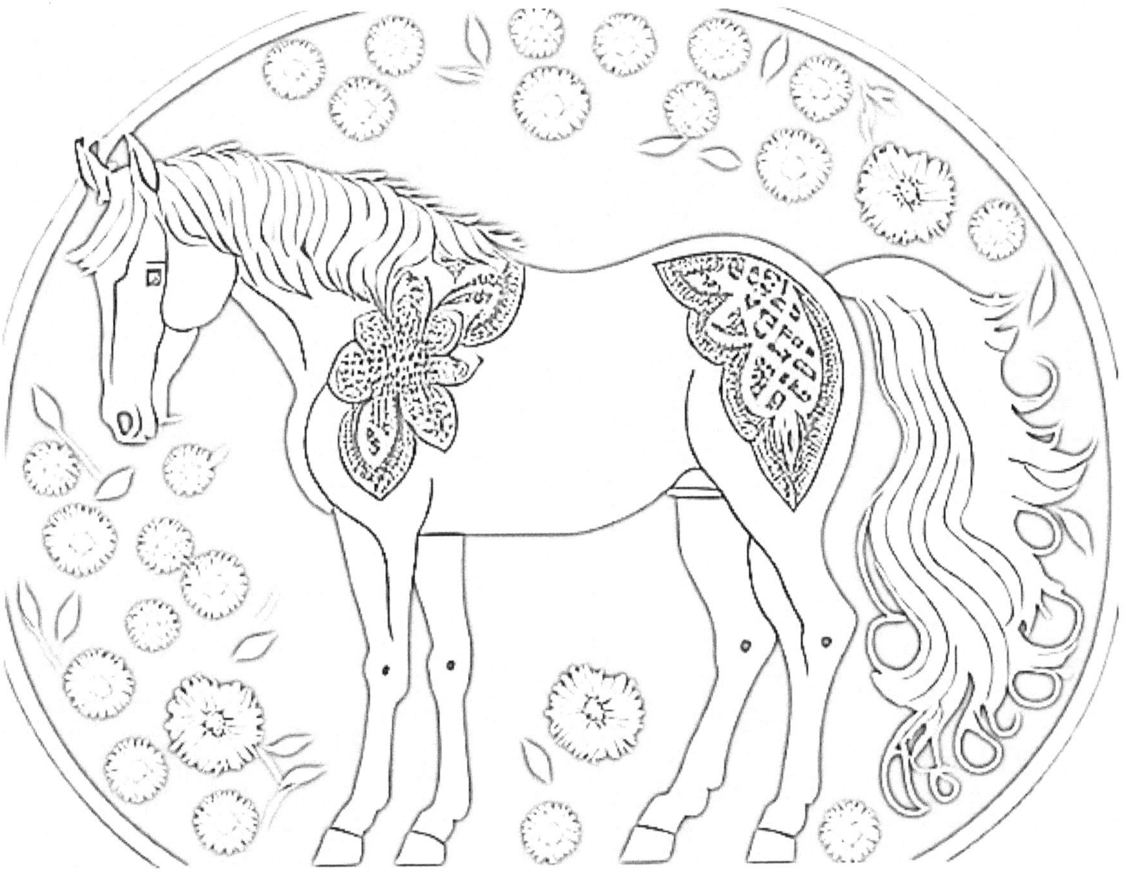

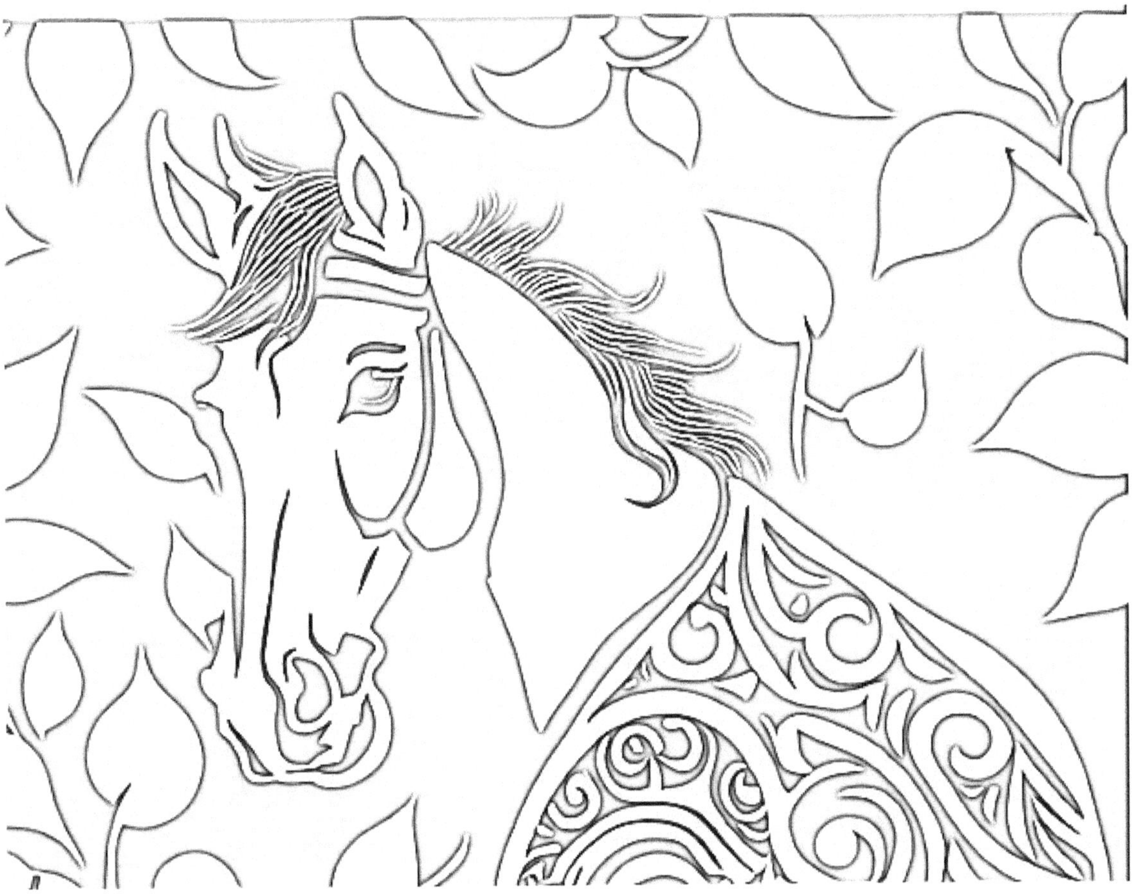

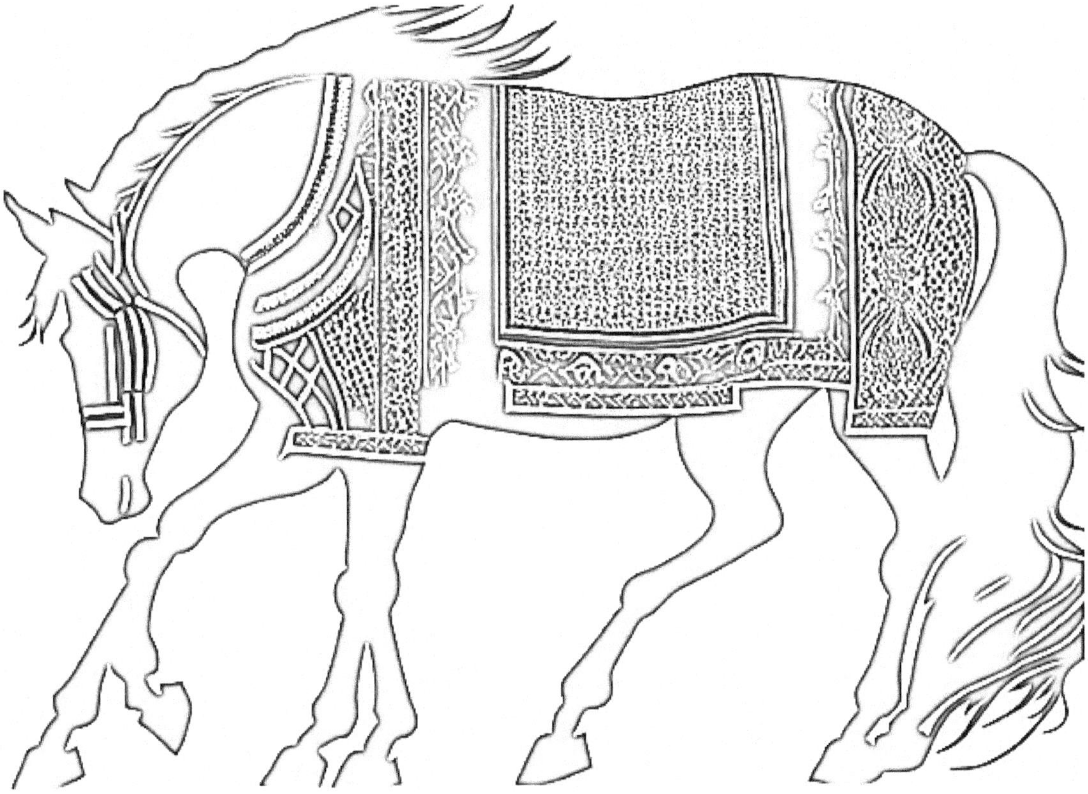

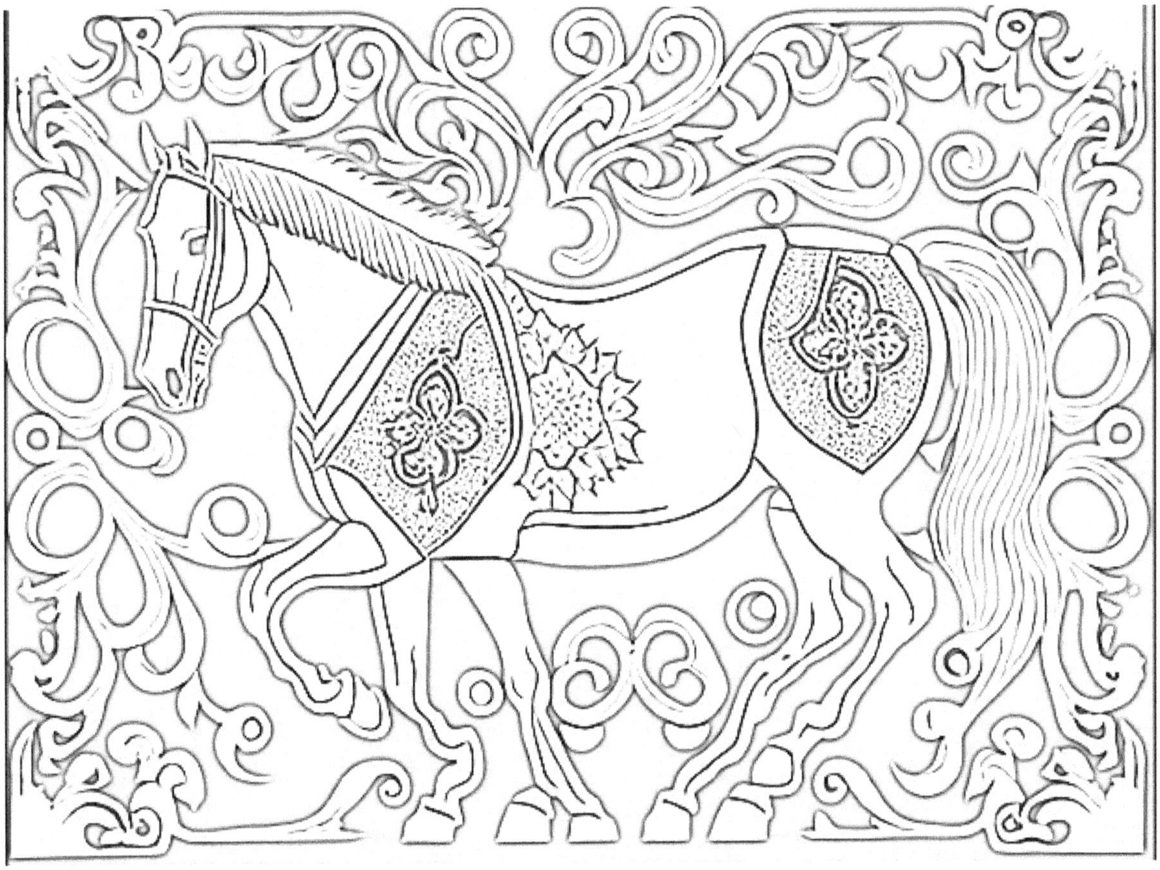

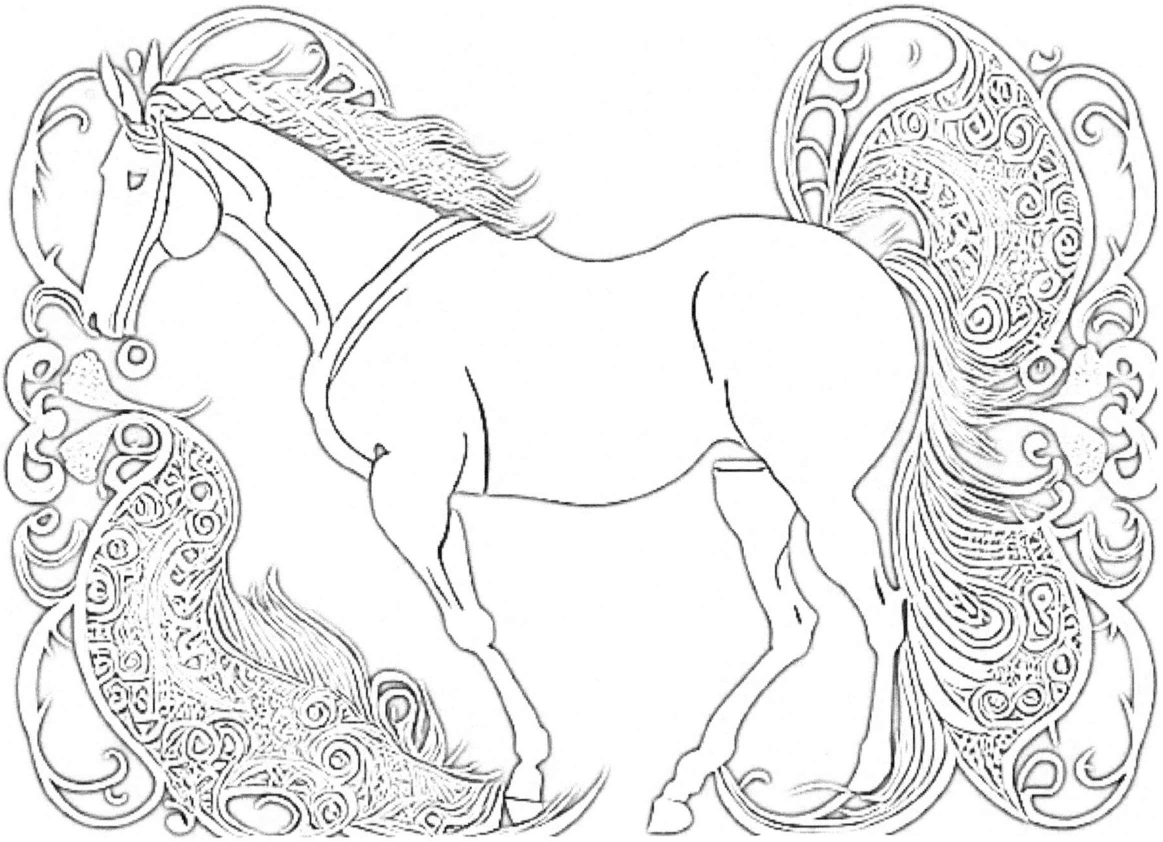

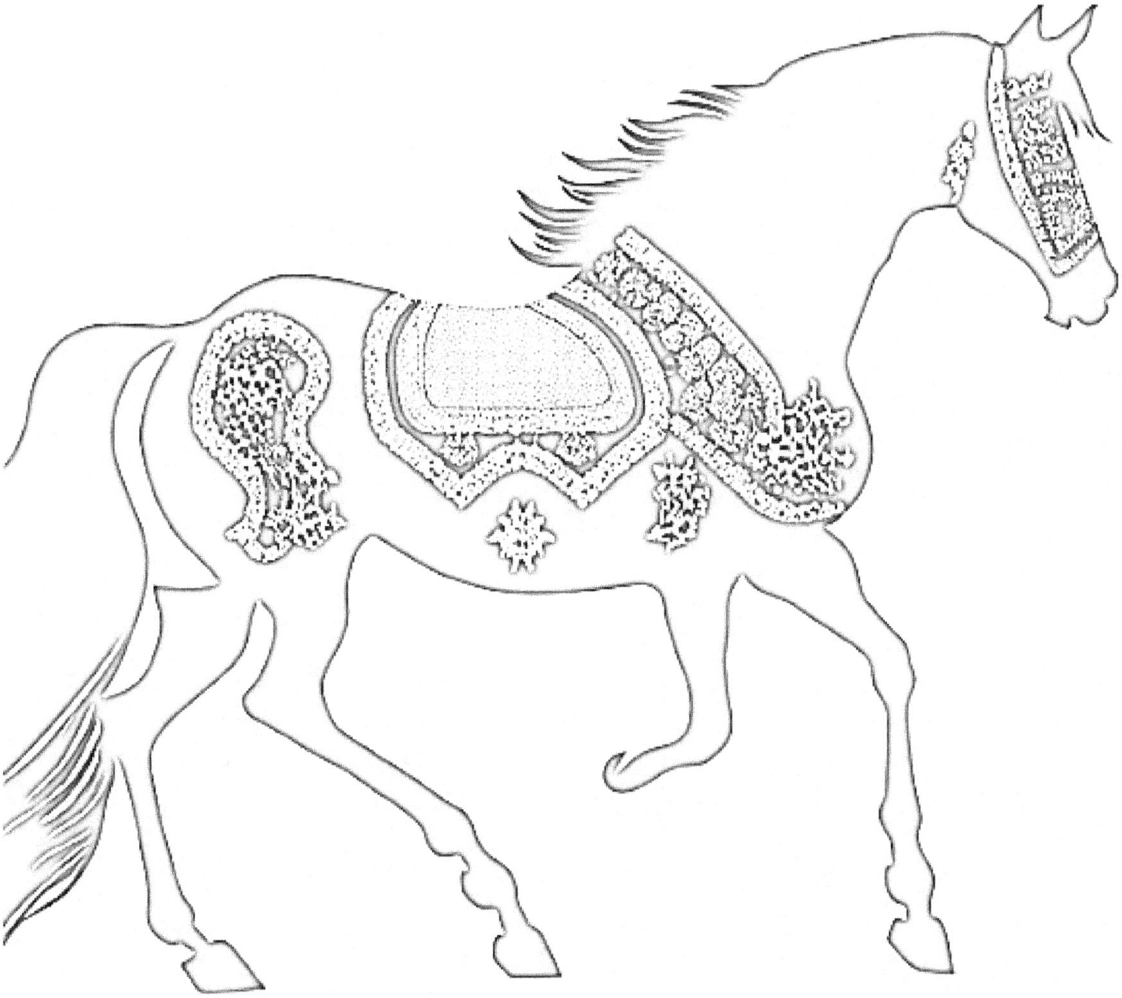

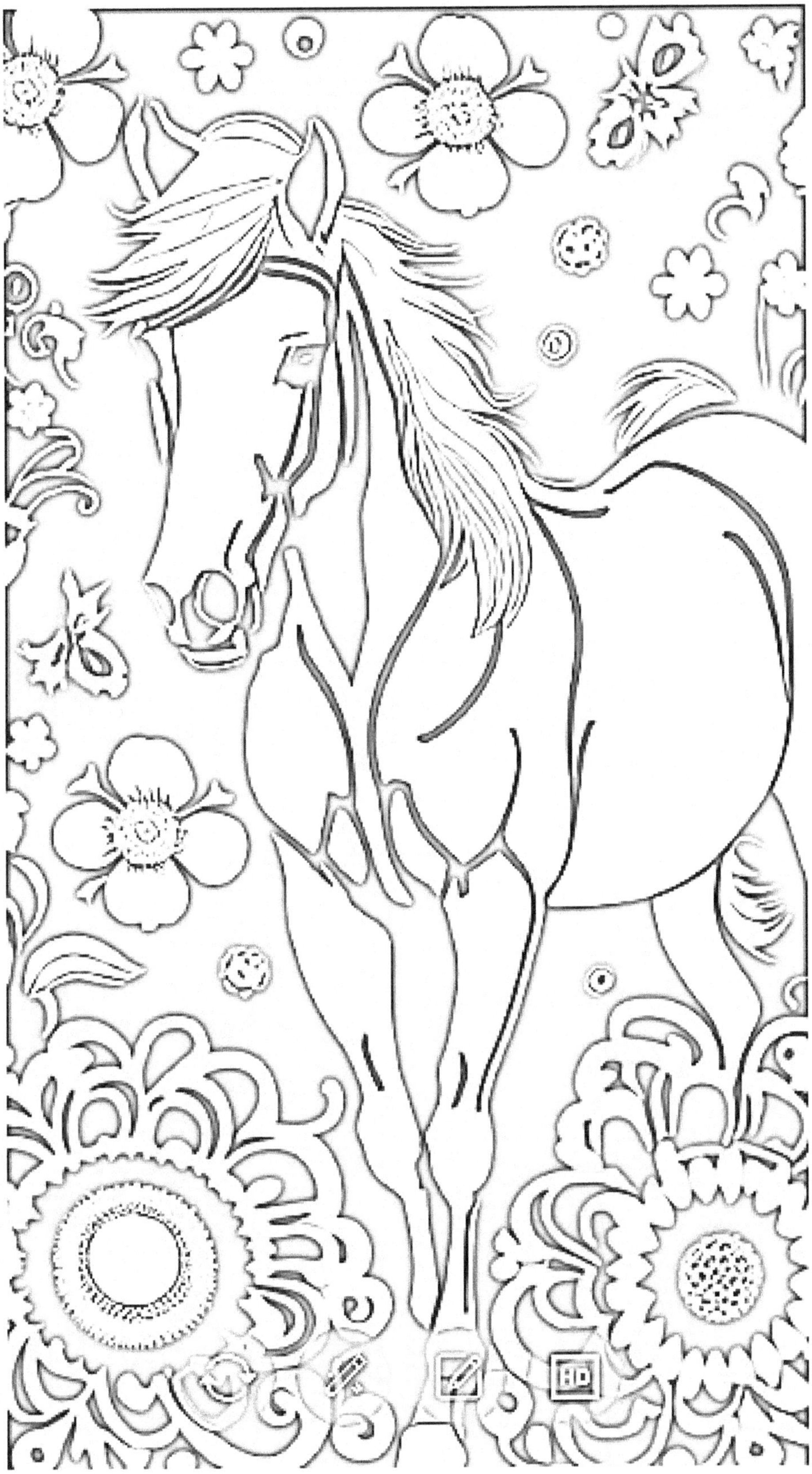

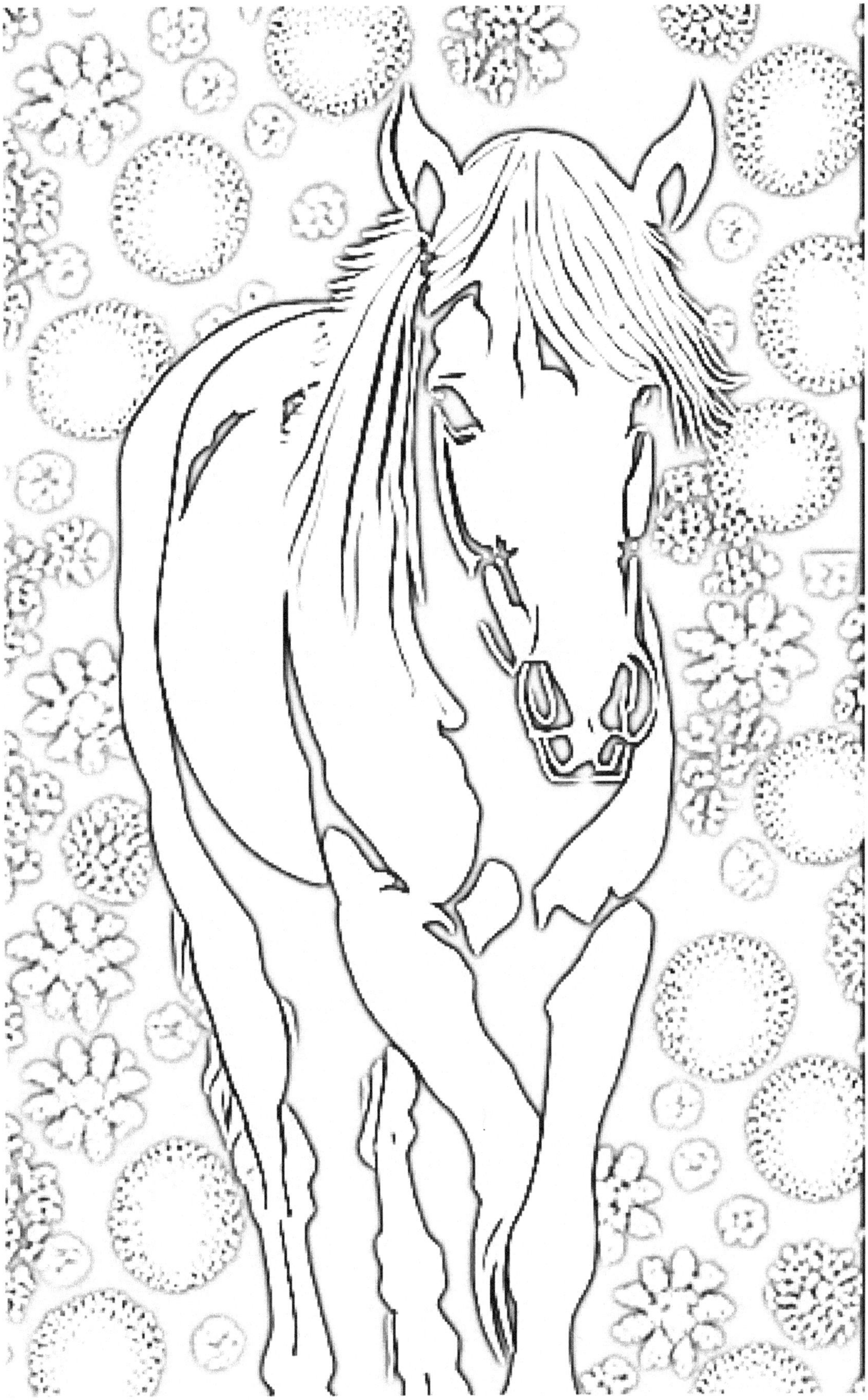

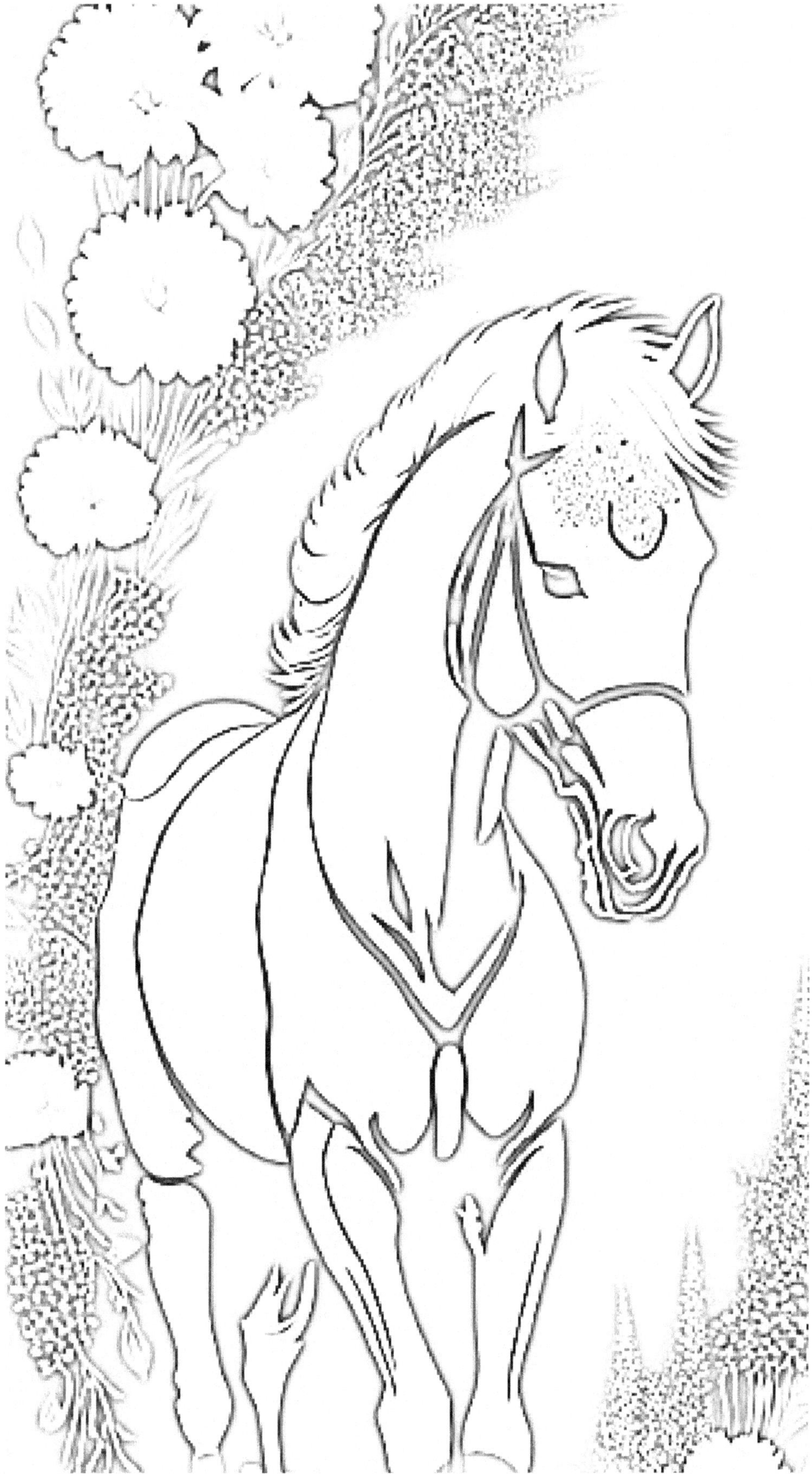

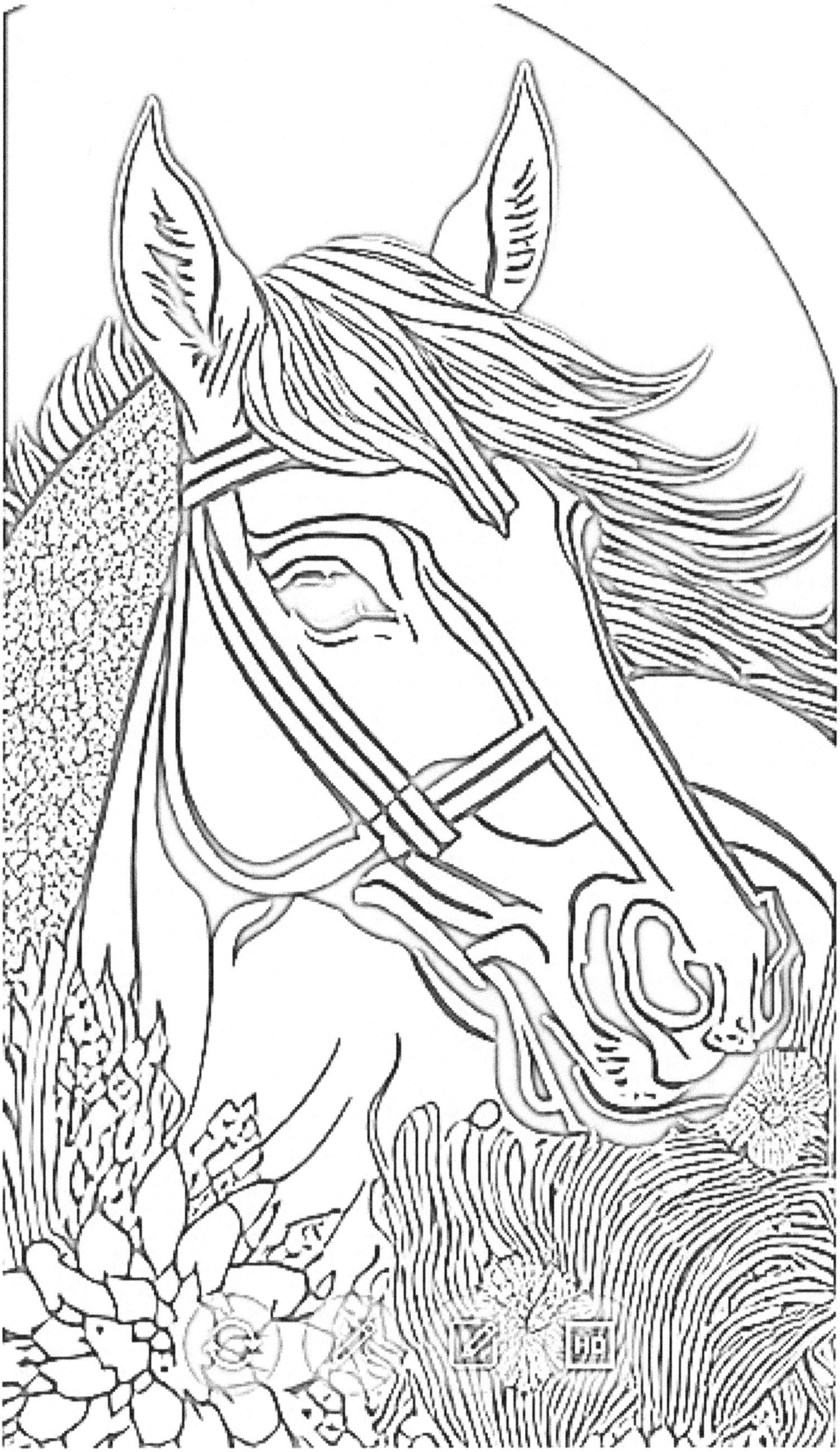

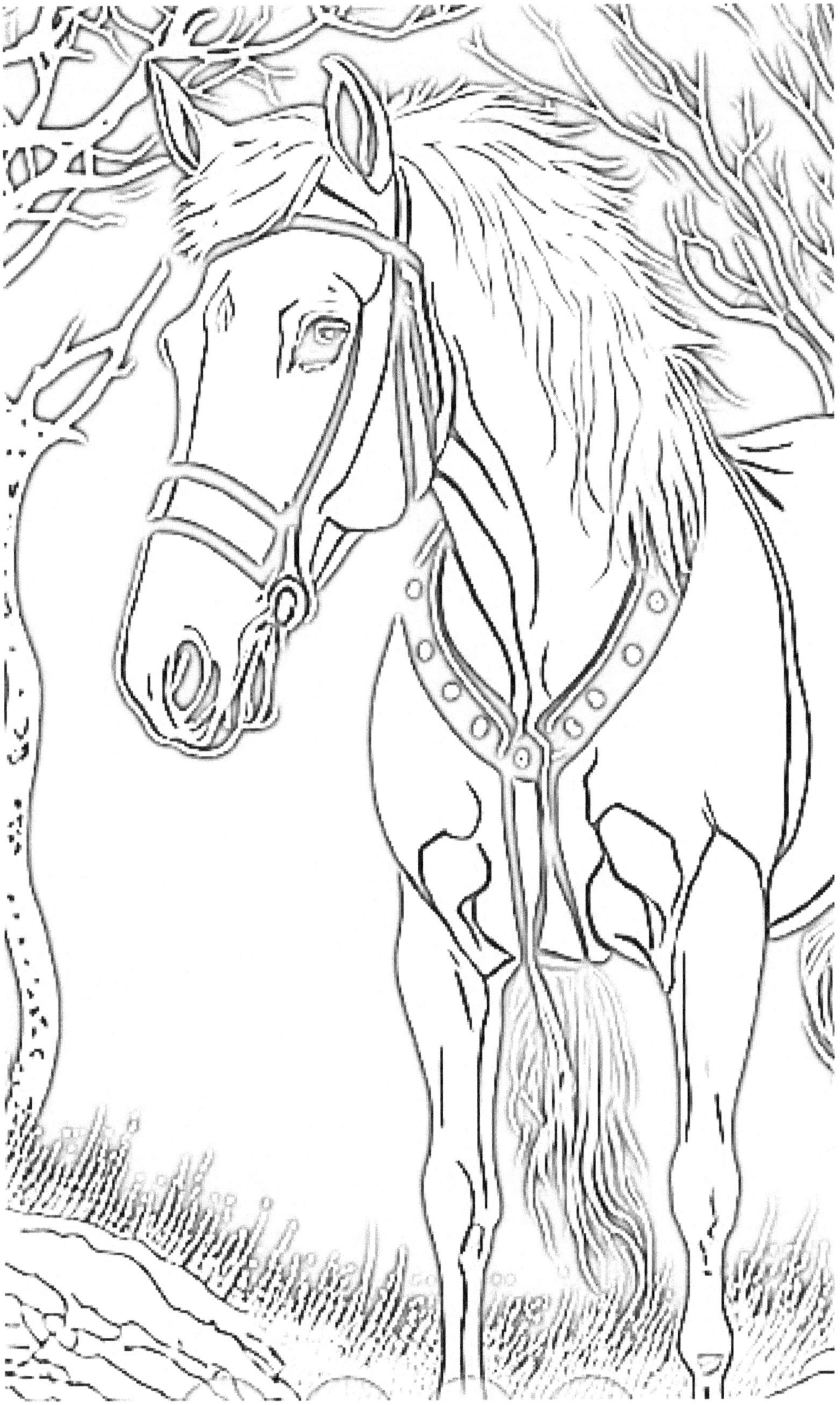

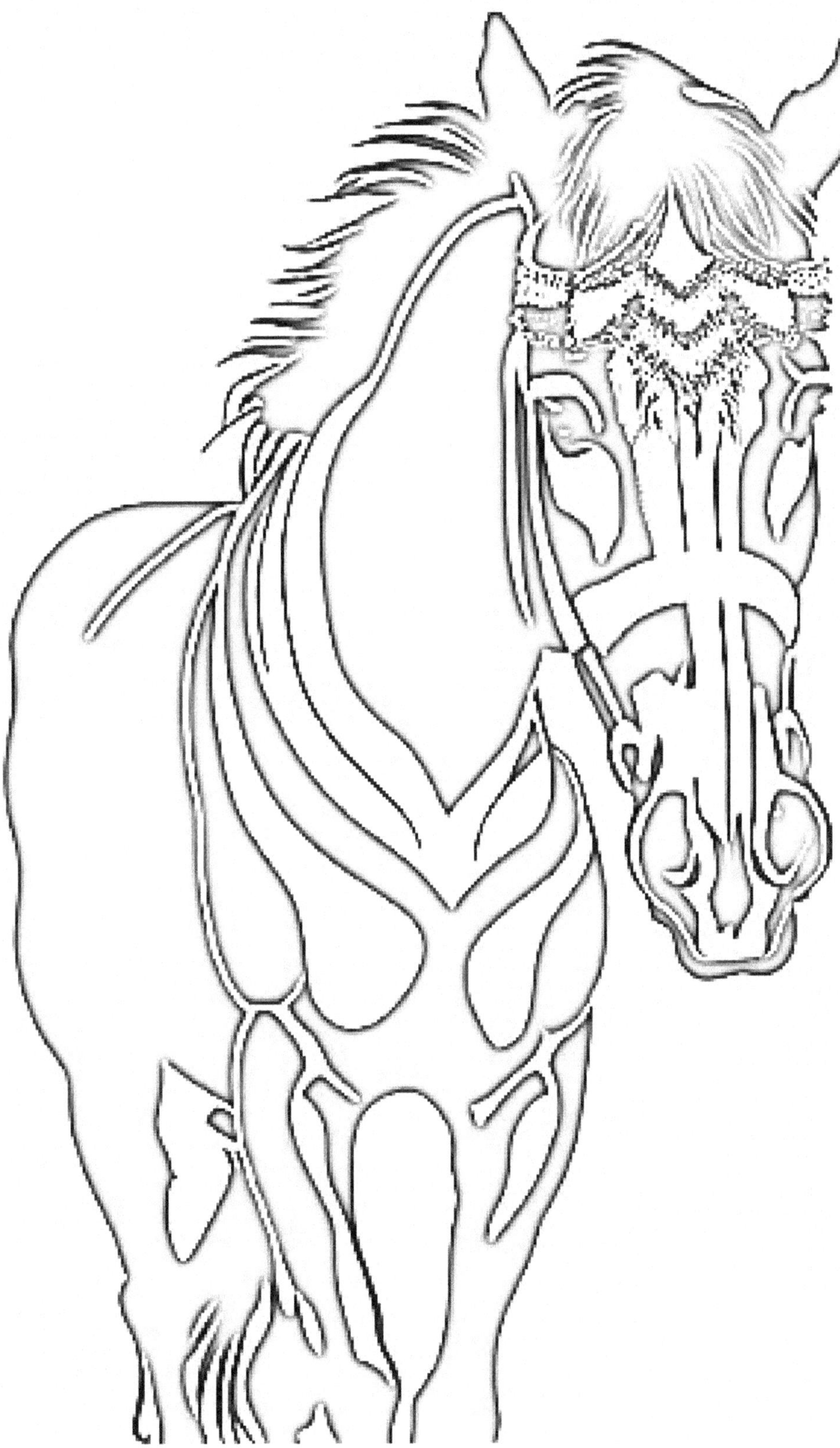

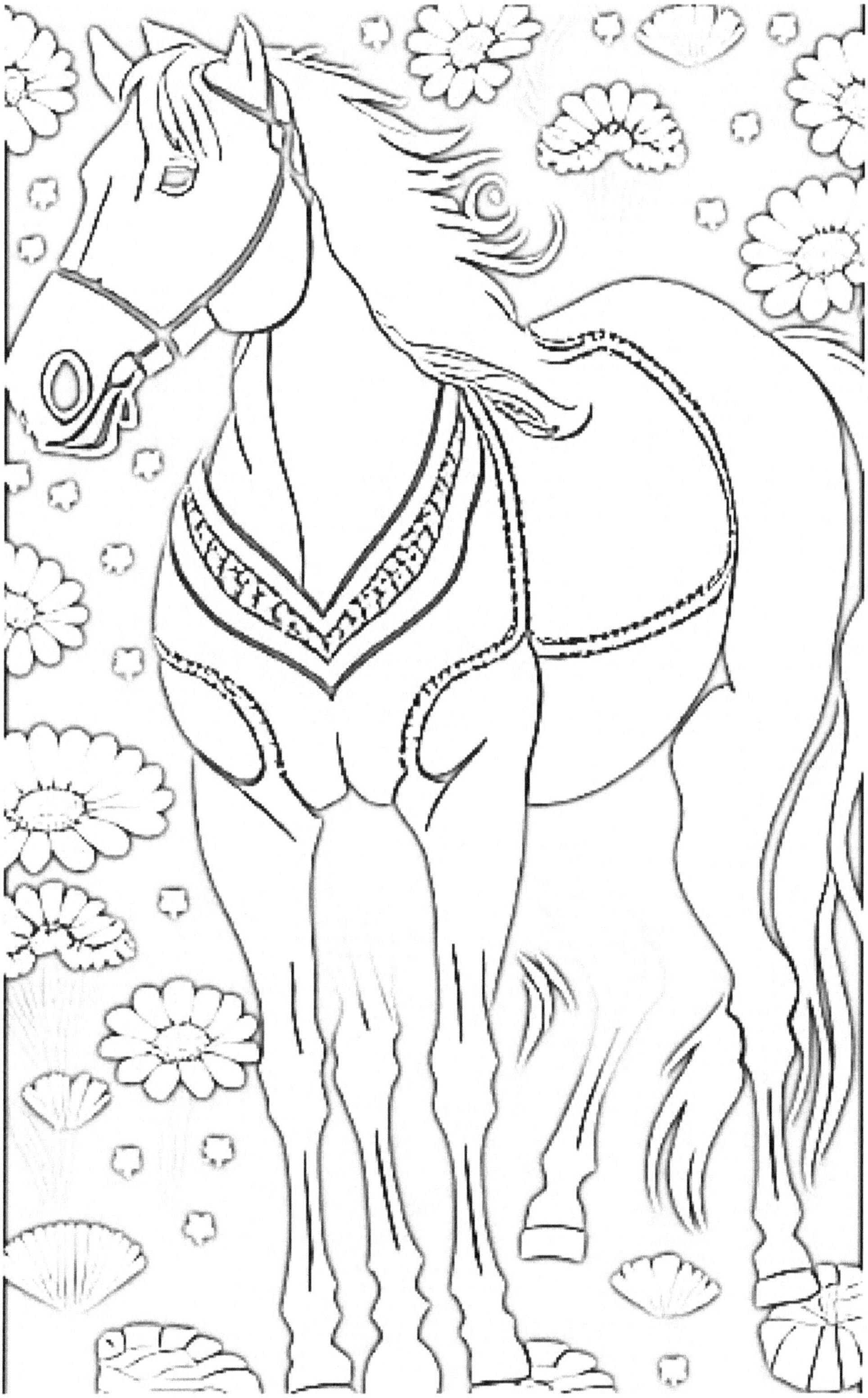

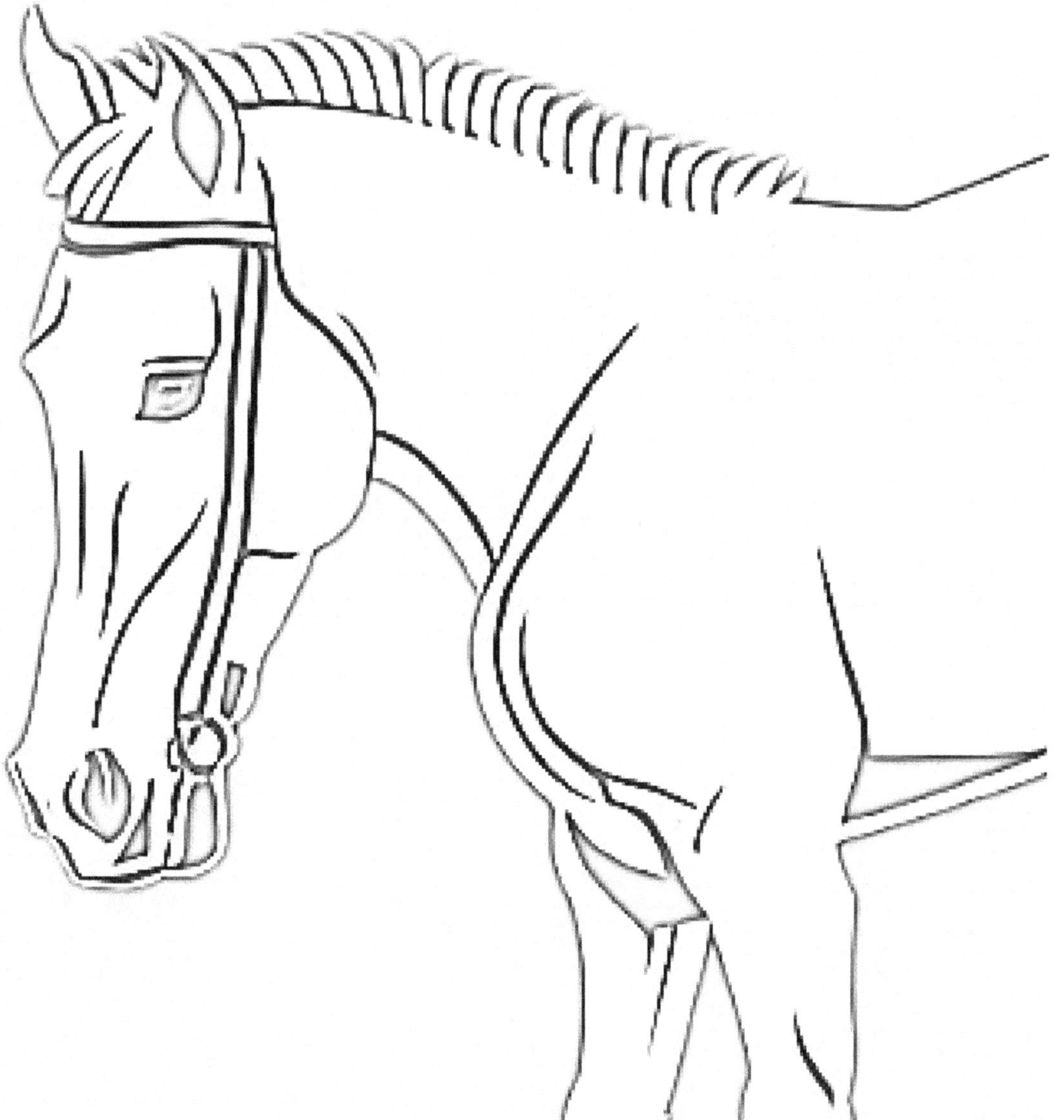

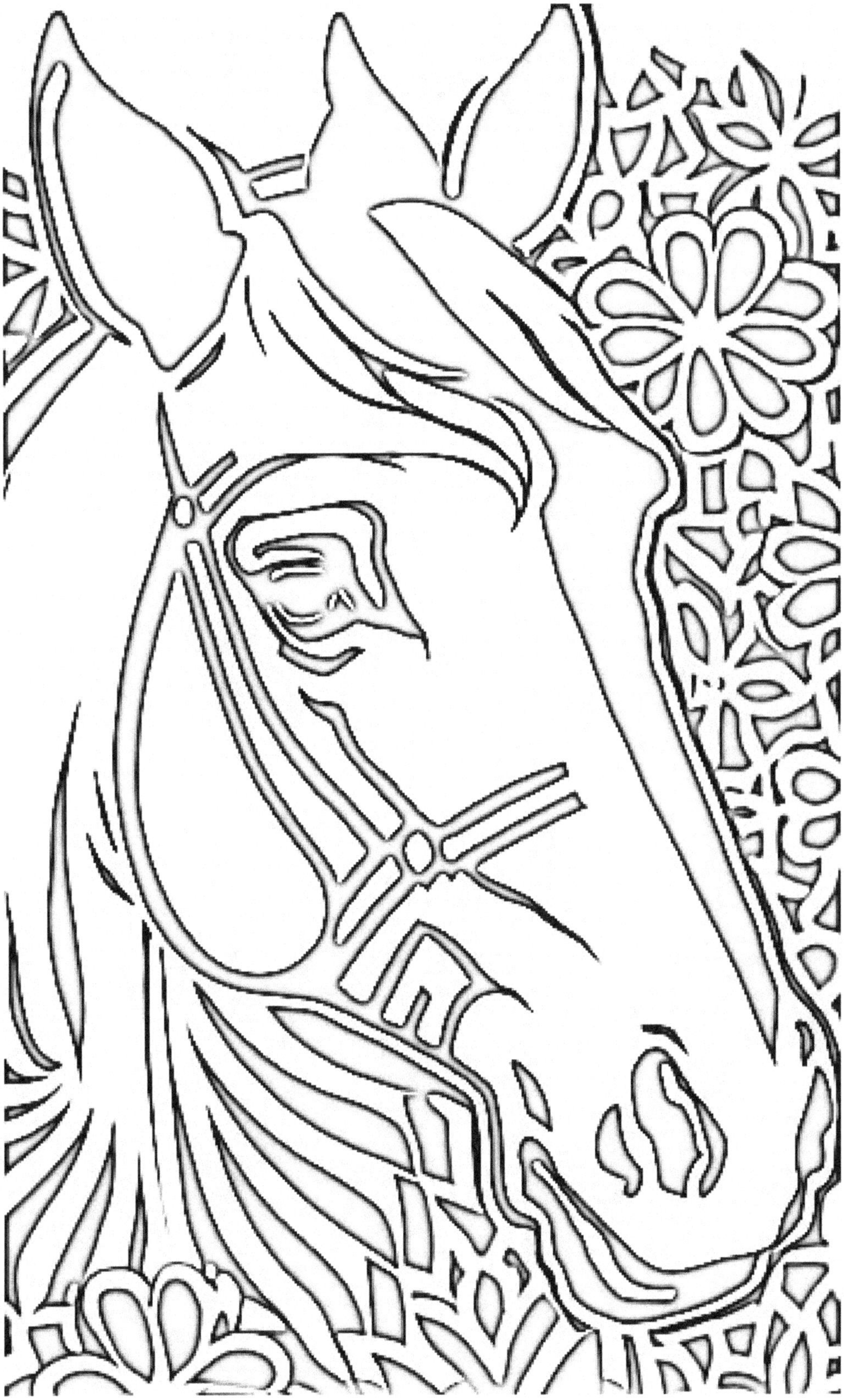

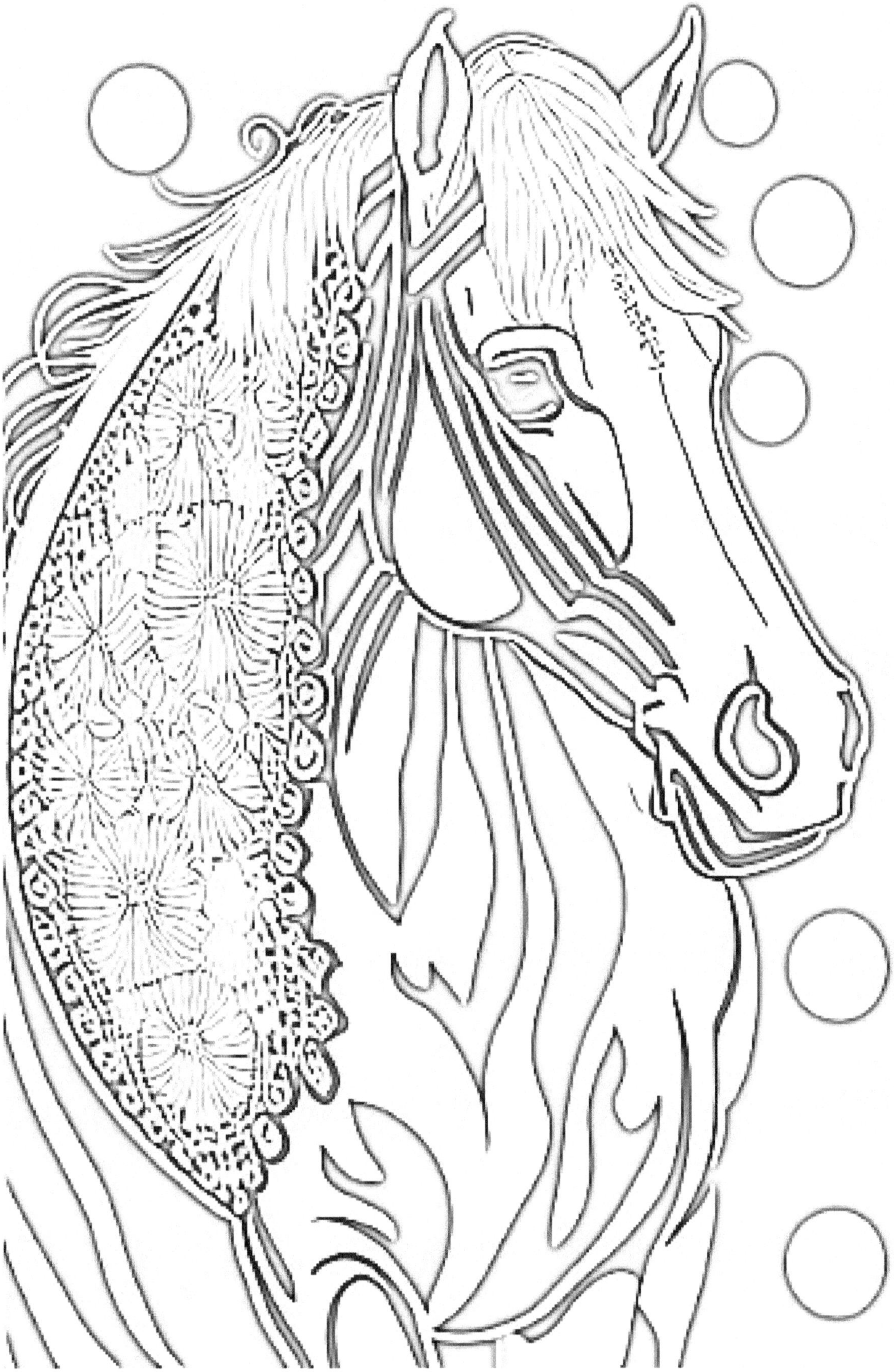

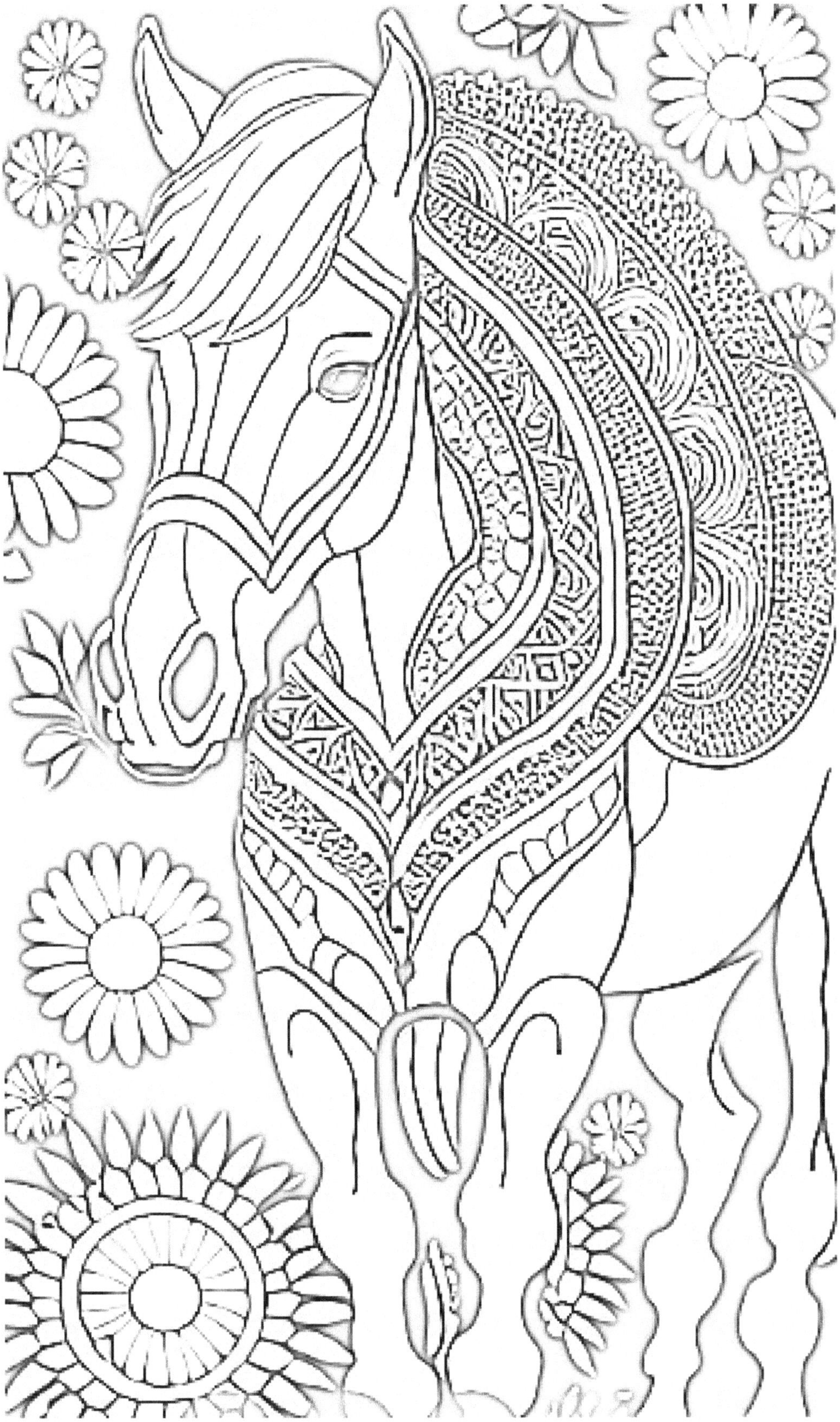

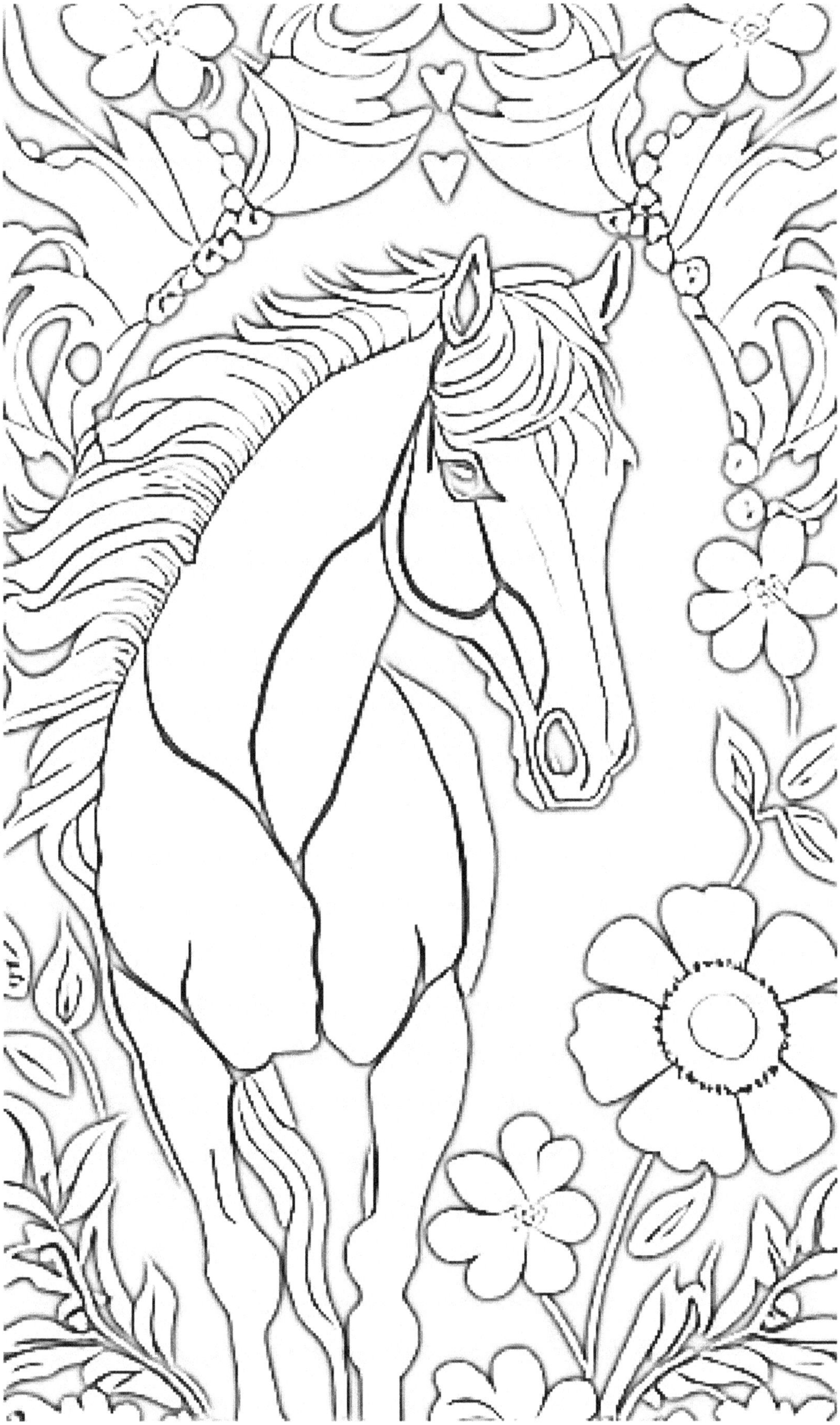

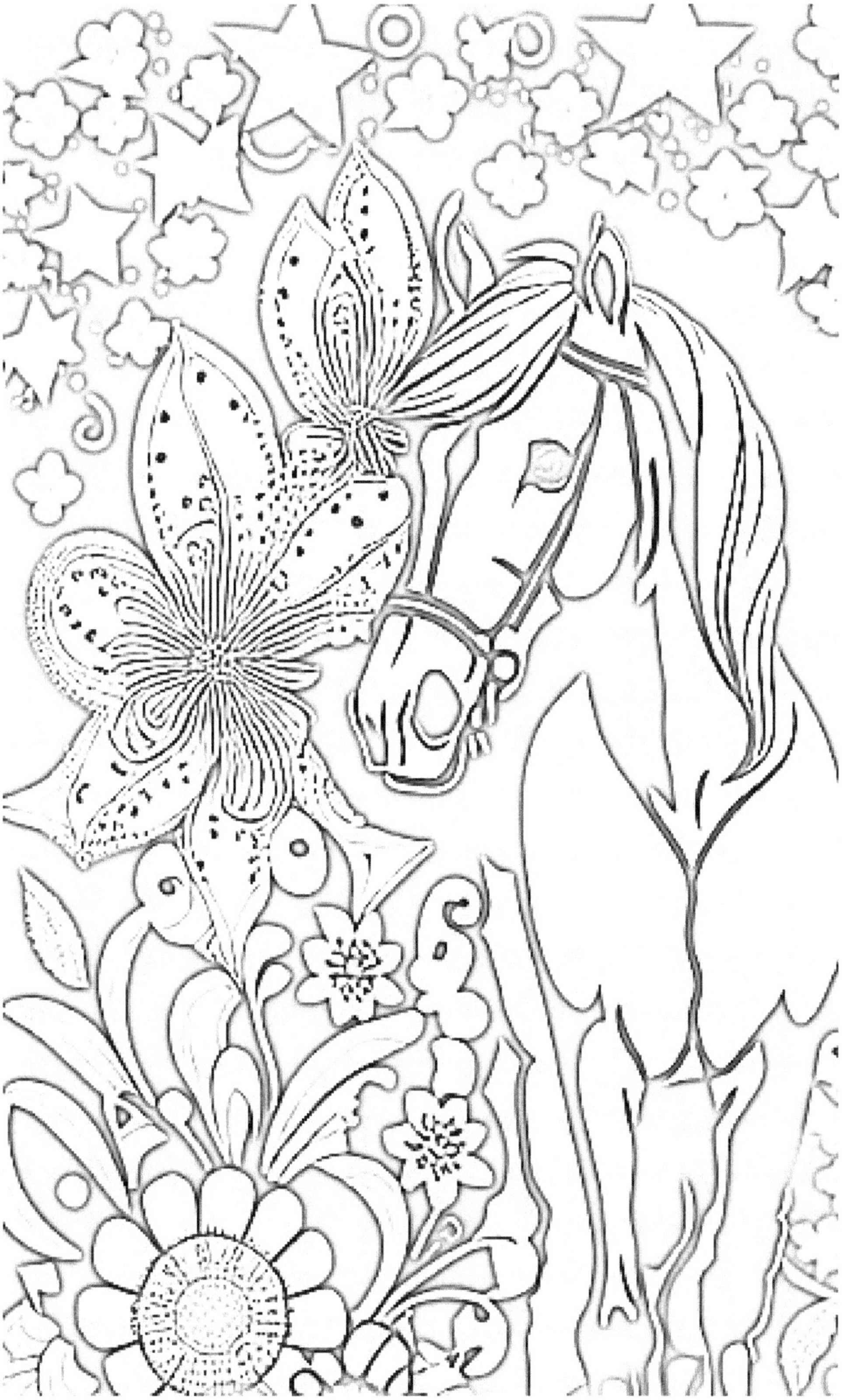

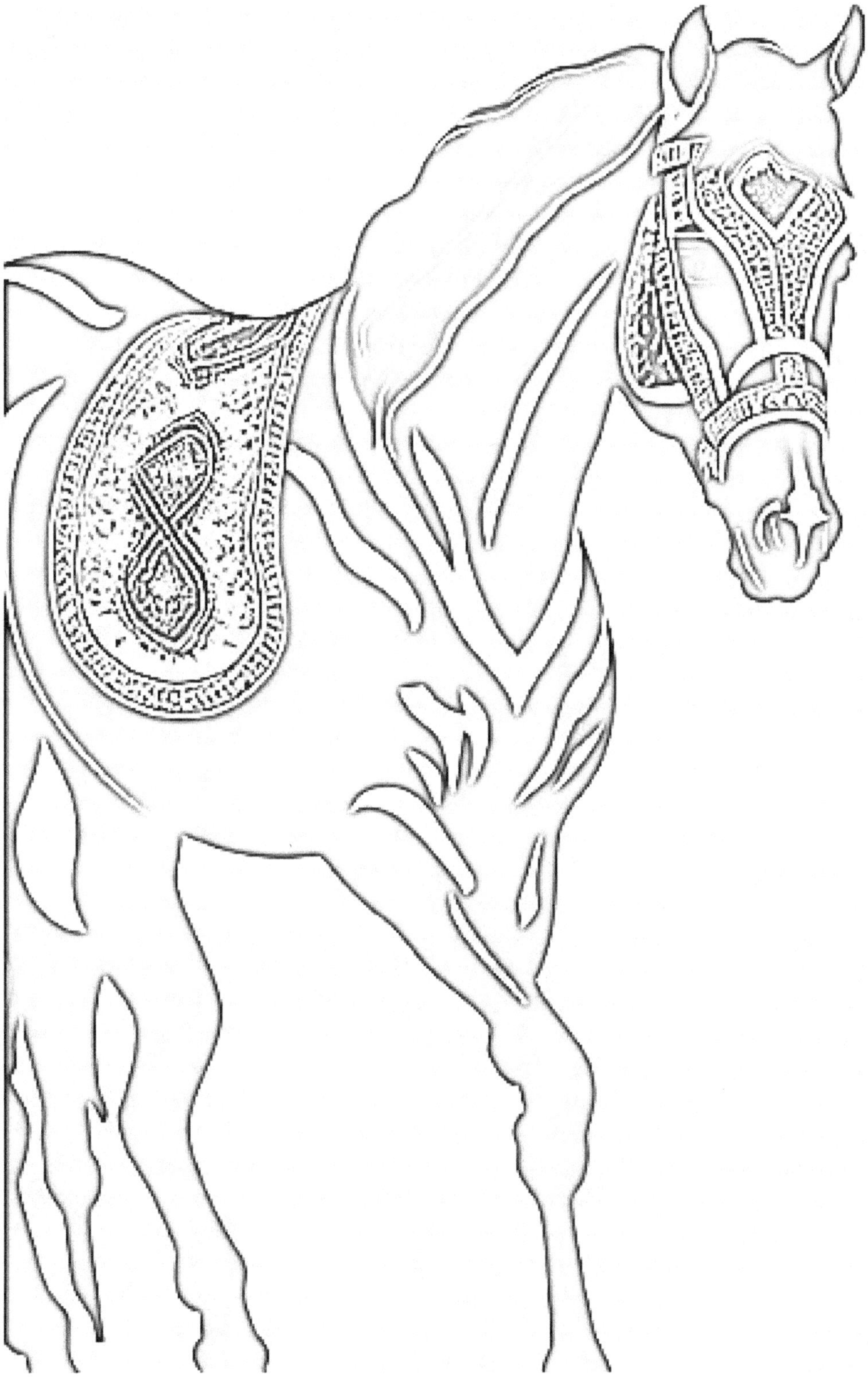

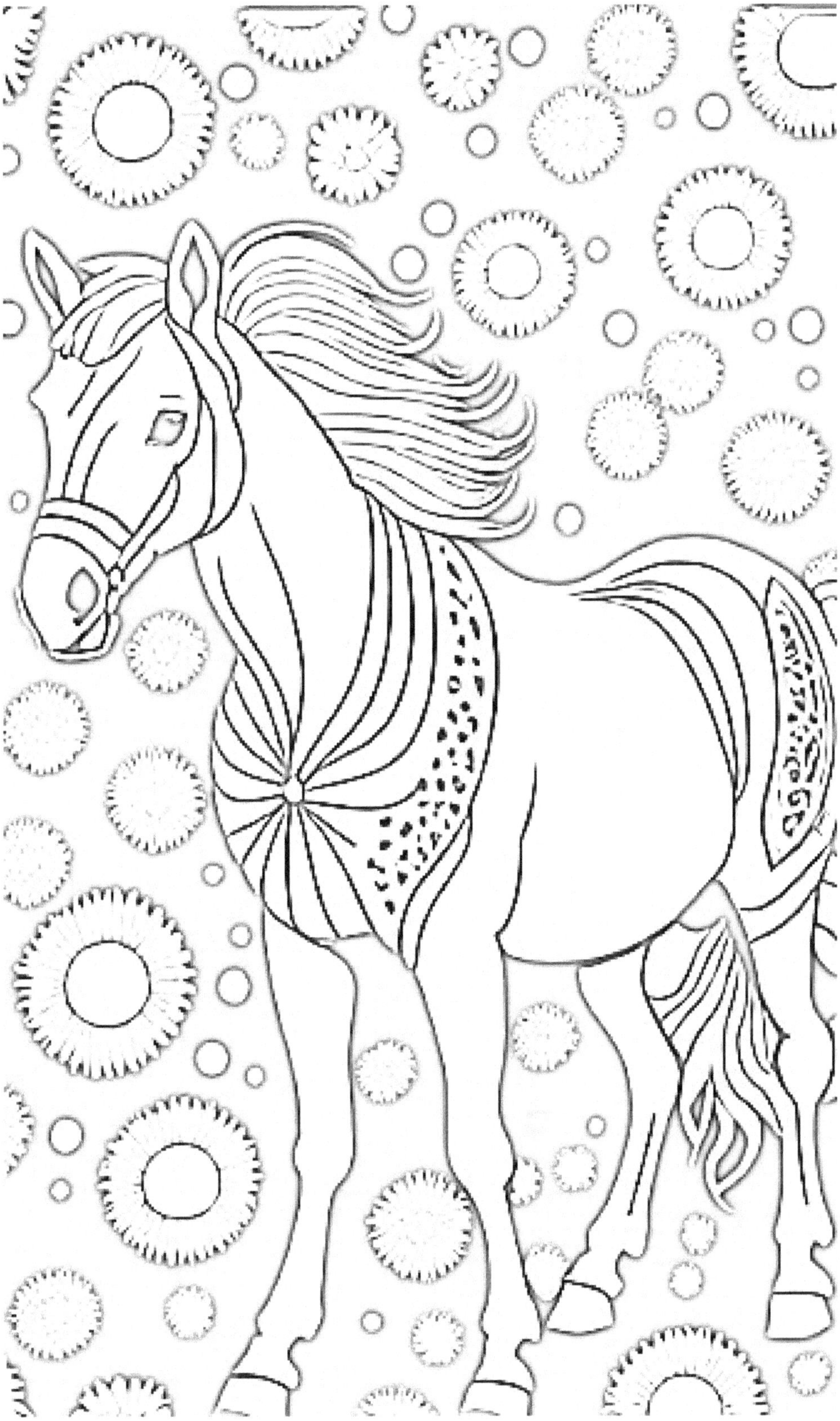

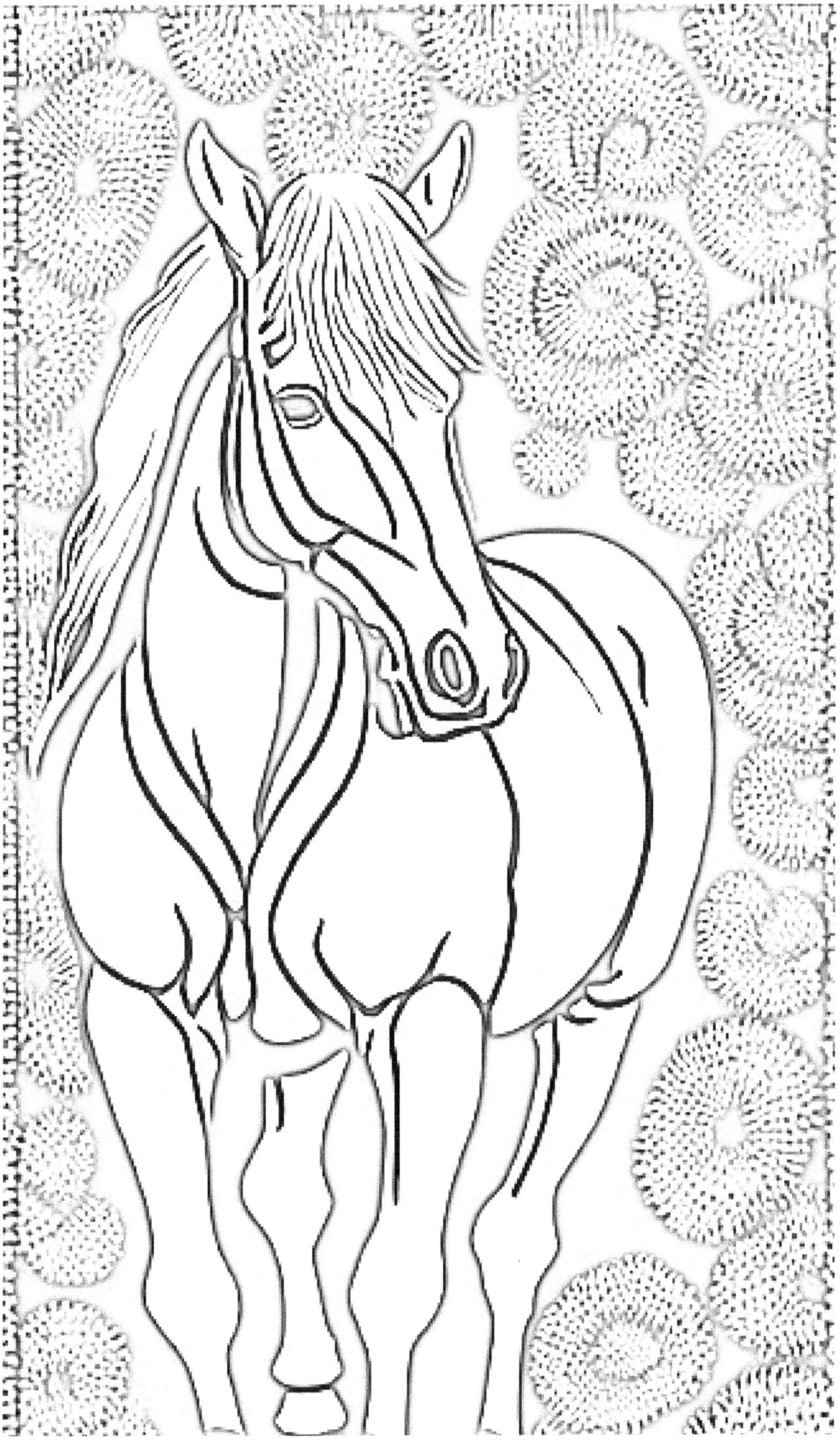

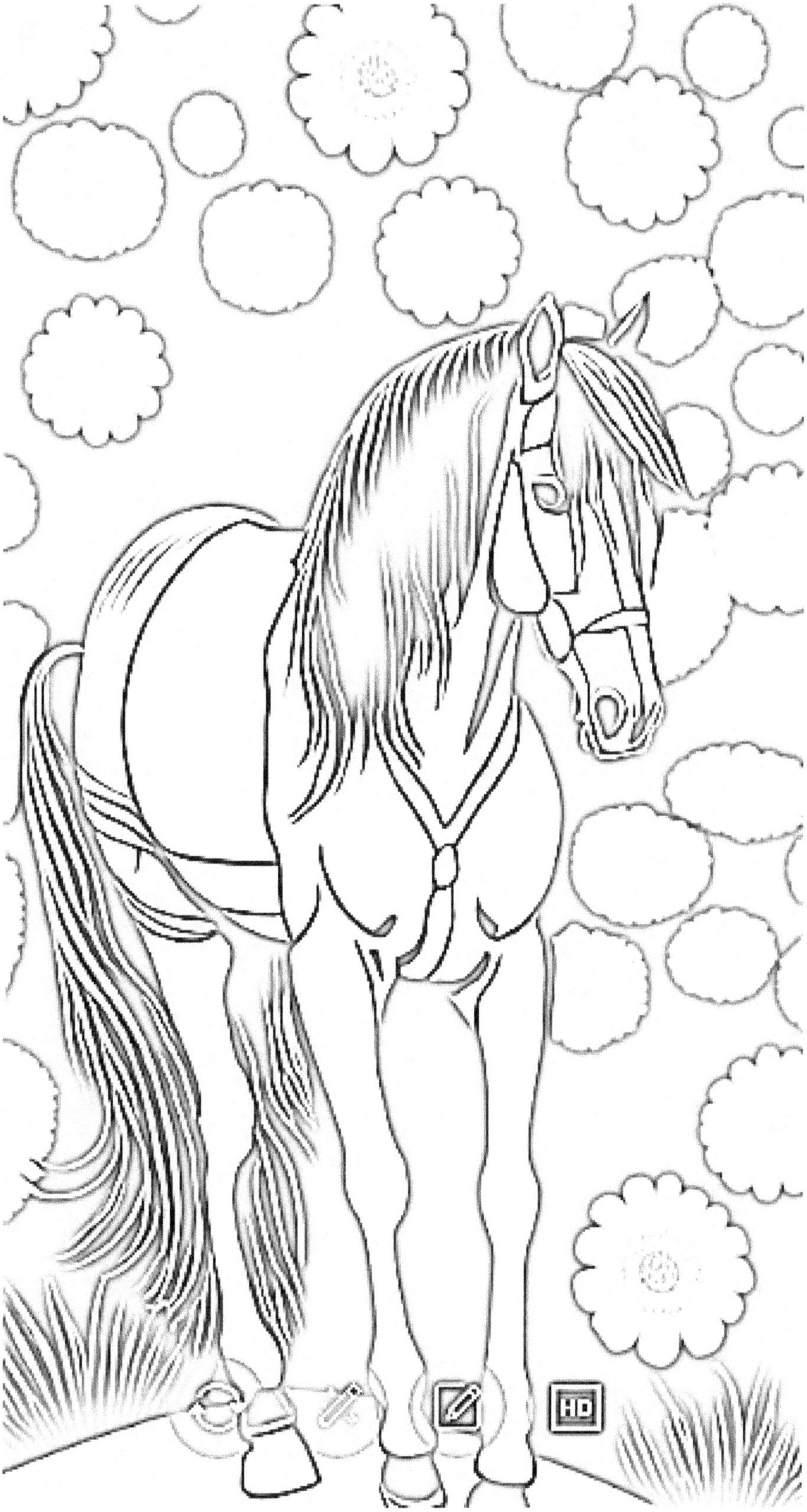
HD

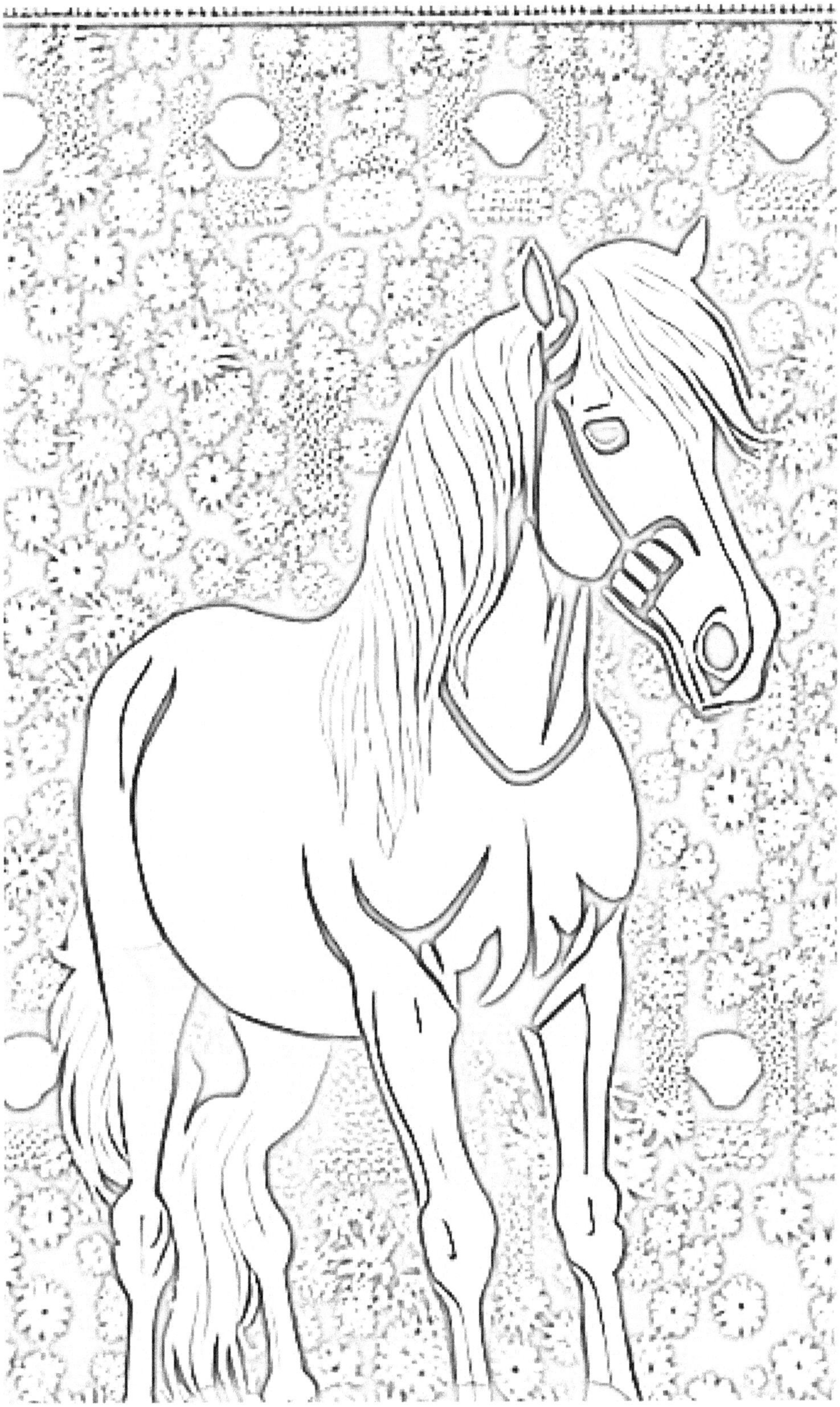

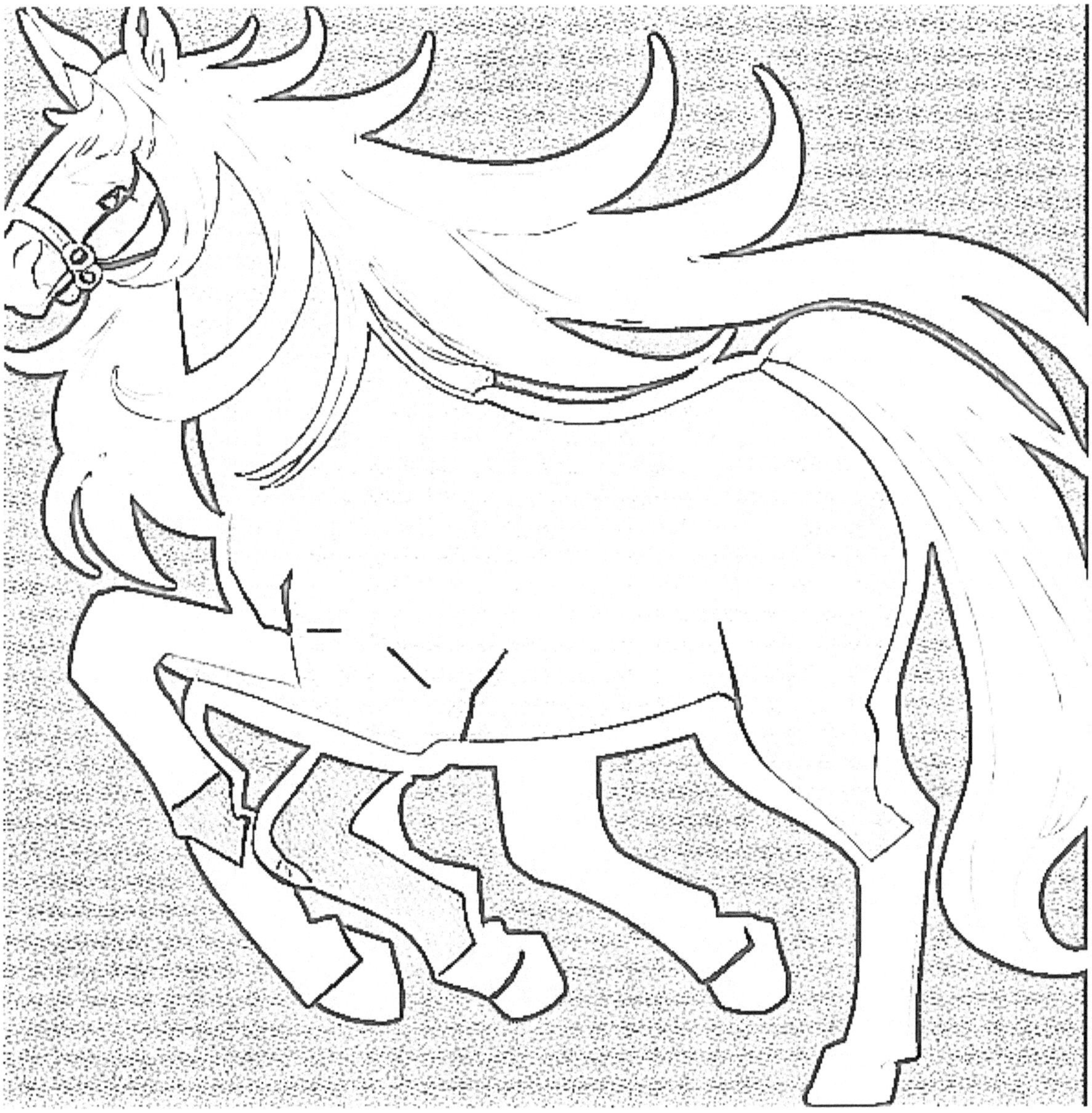

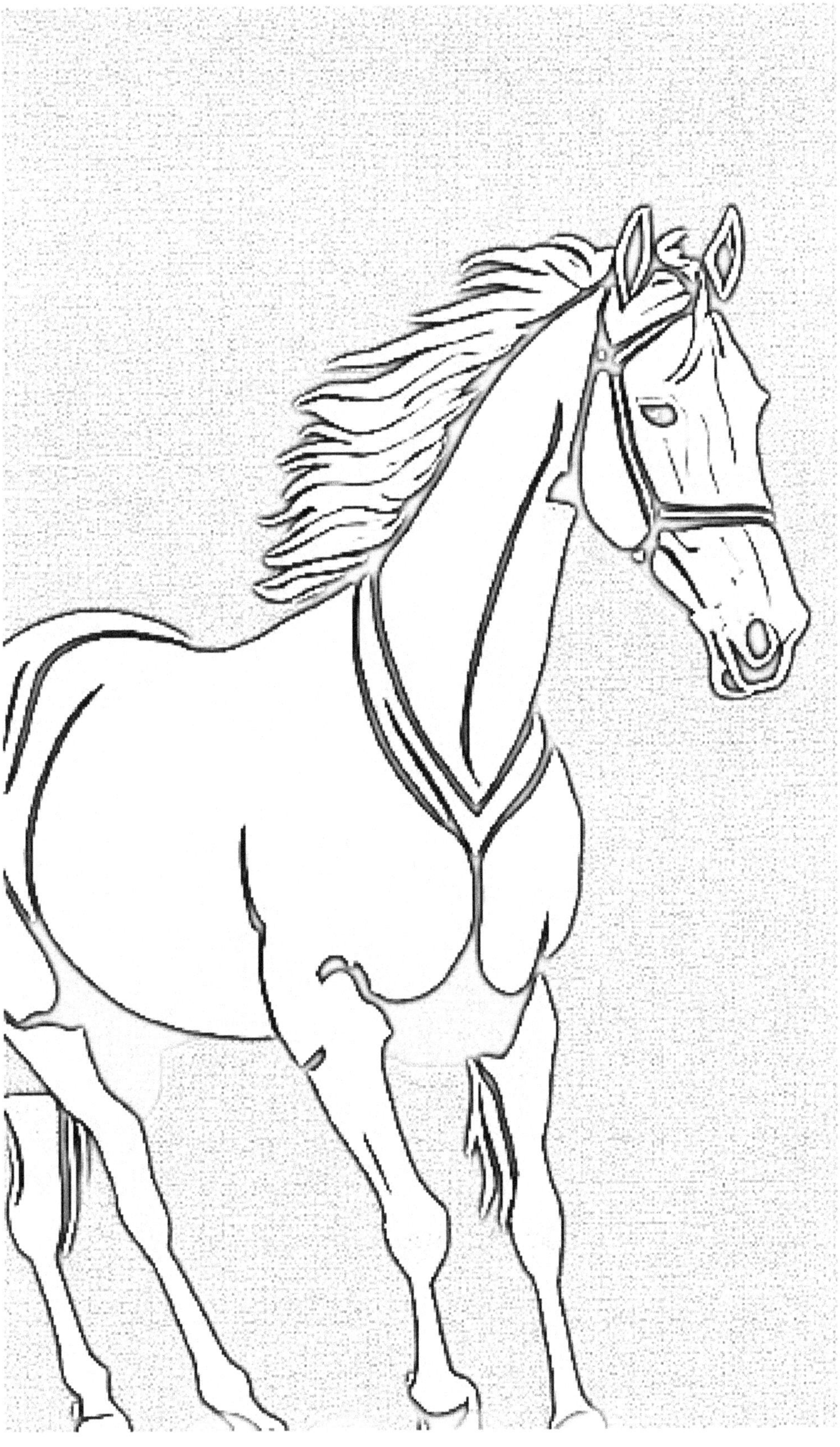

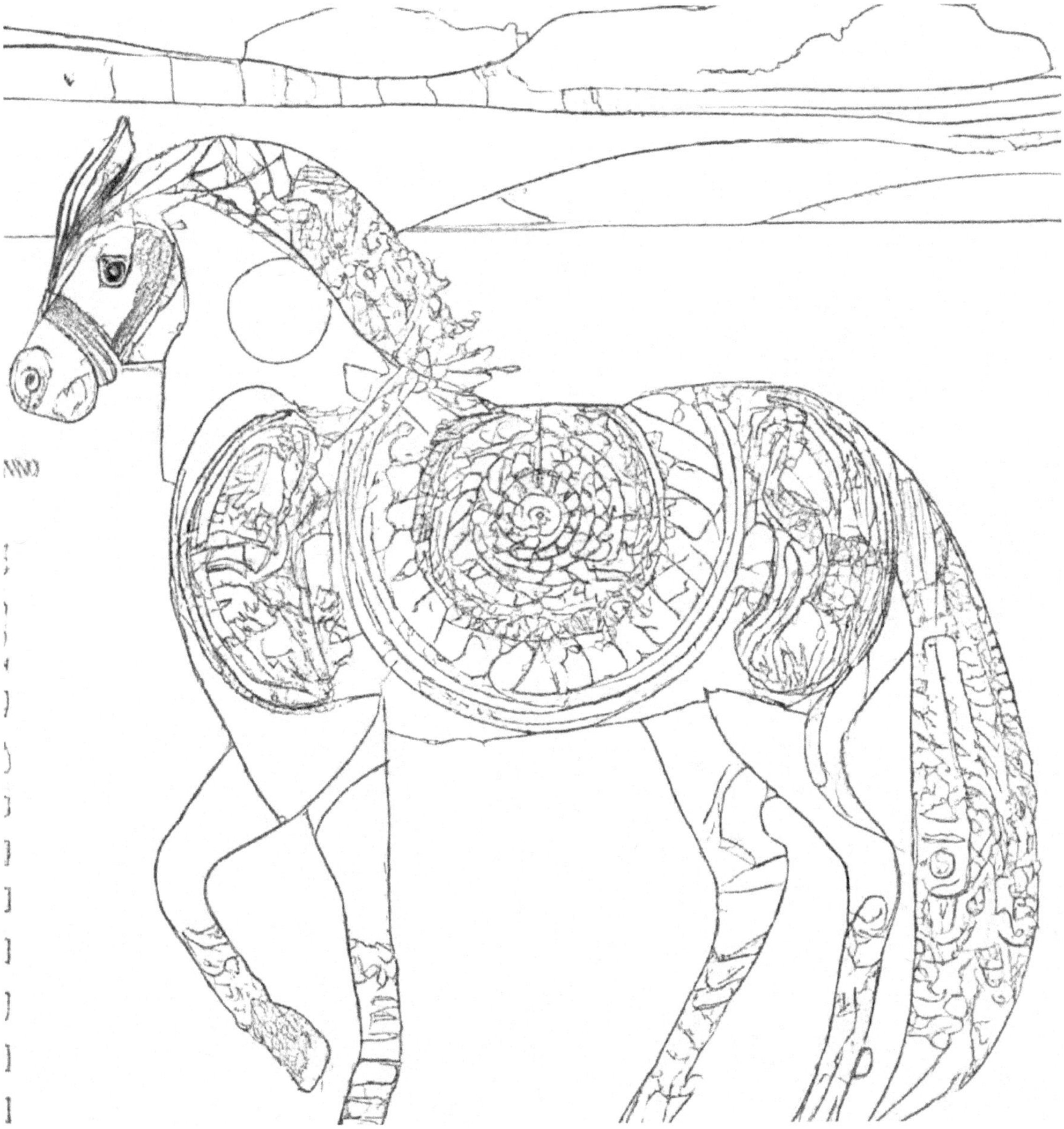

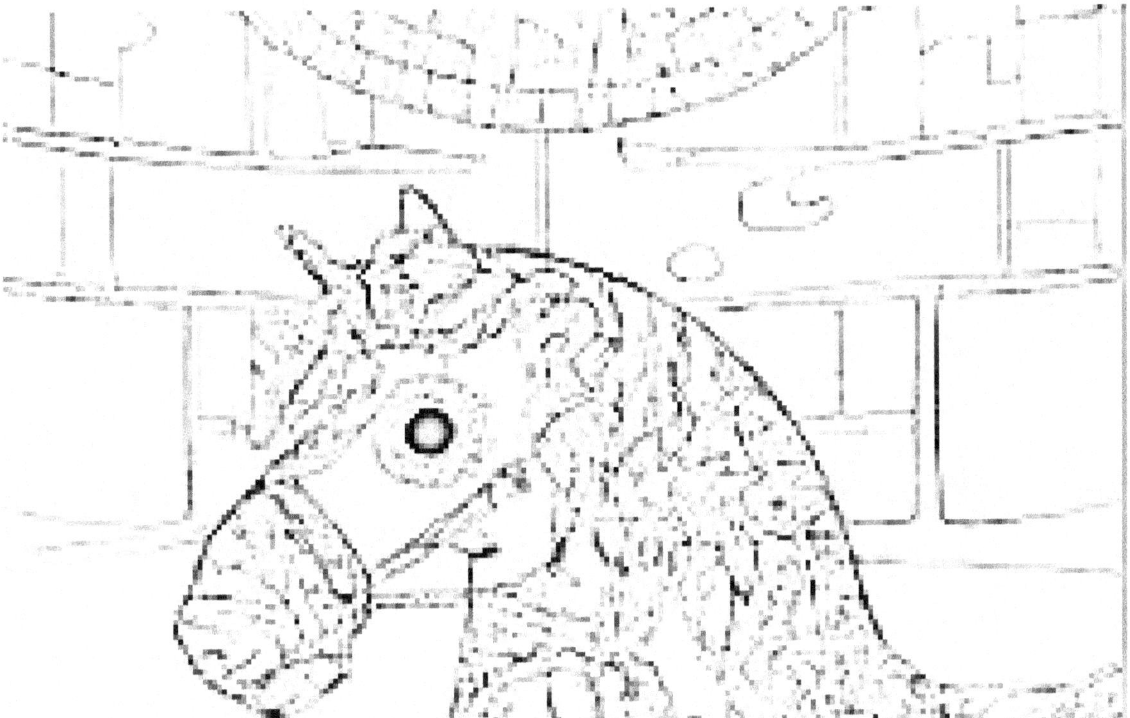

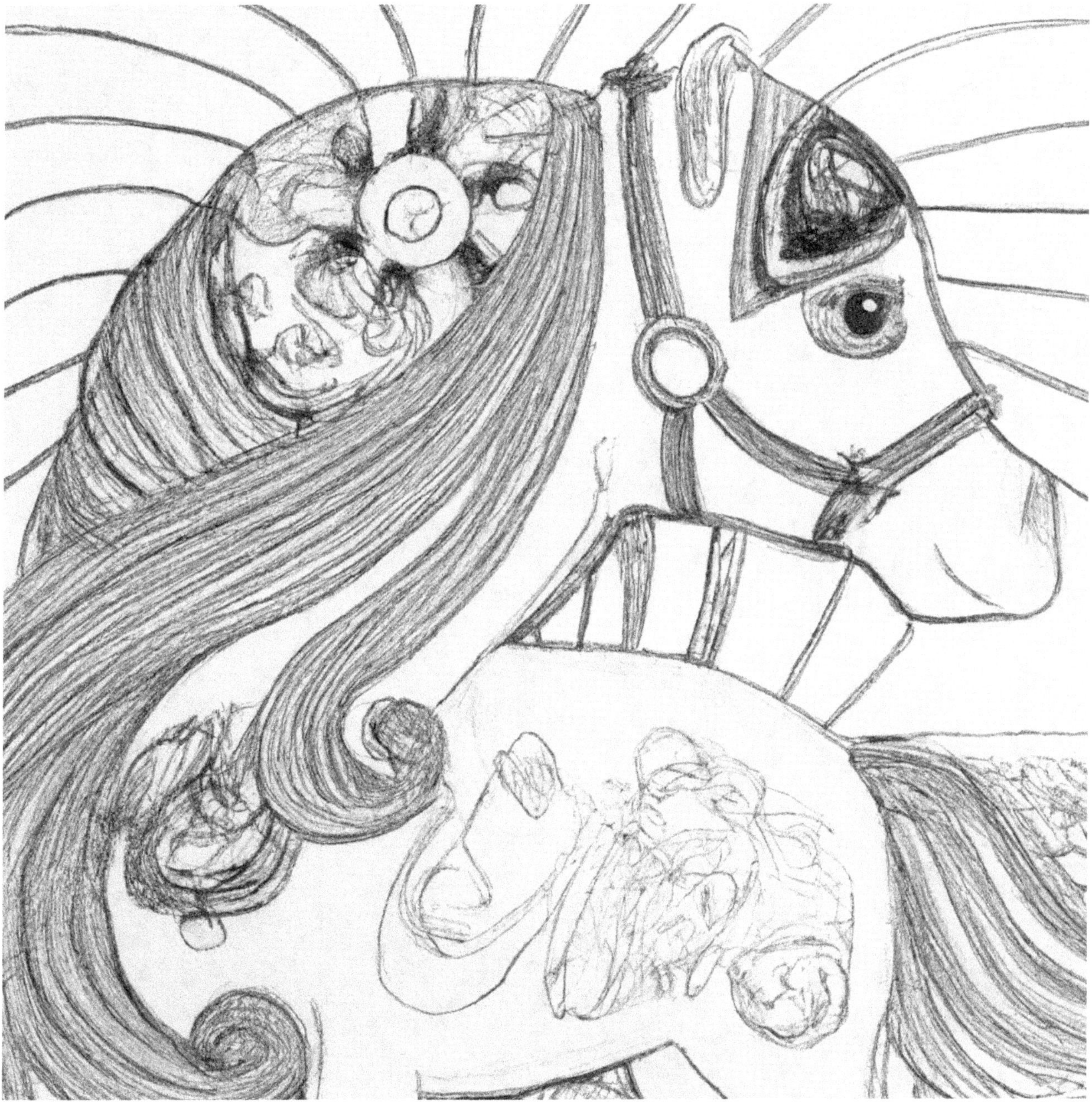

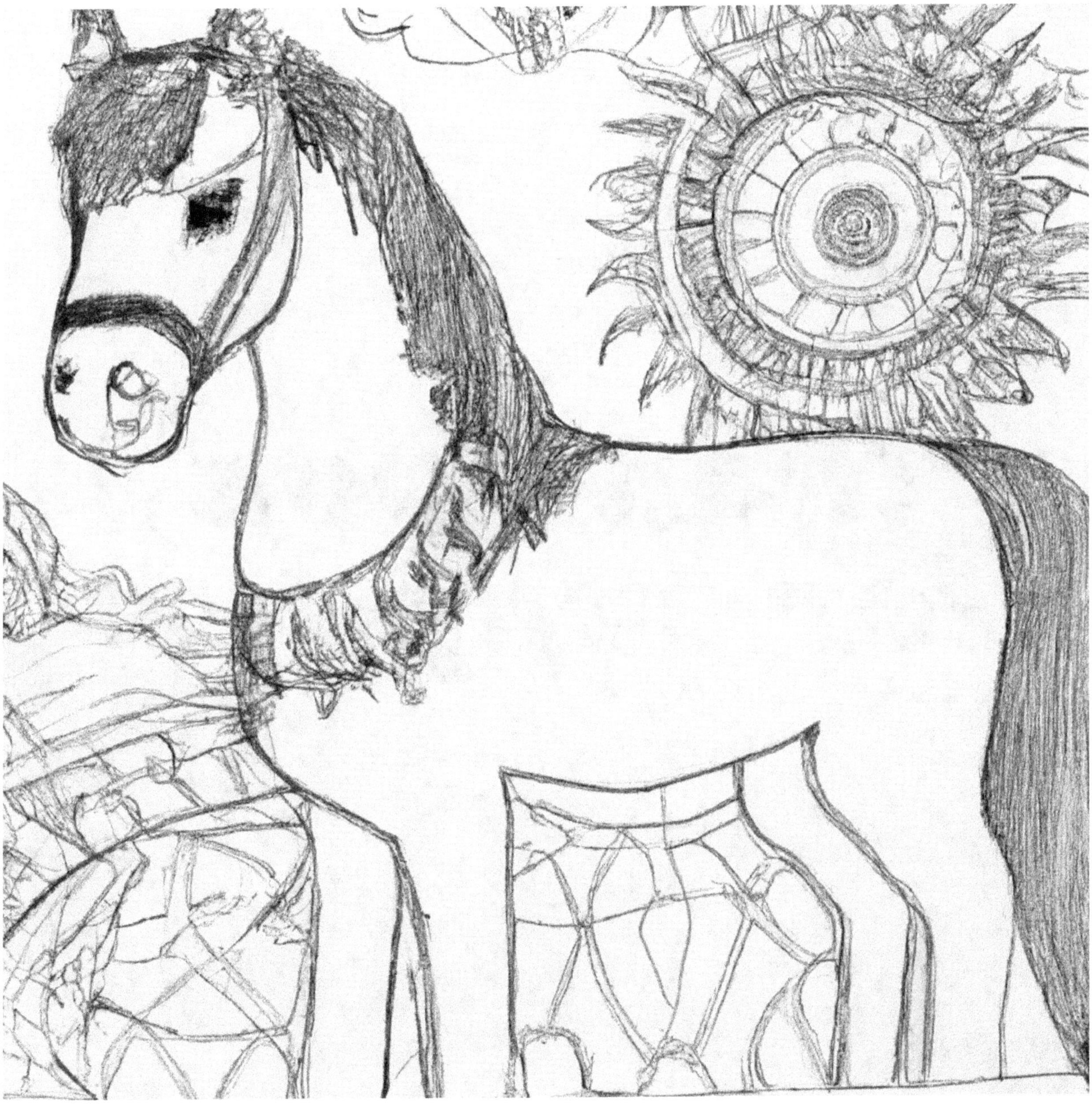

thank you
for support!

www.ingramcontent.com/pod-product-compliance
Lightning Source LLC
Chambersburg PA
CBHW082152230526
45467CB00044B/2947
9798386692711